KS3
MATHS
REVISION GUIDE

GILLIAN RICH

About this Book

Whether you learn best by seeing, hearing or doing (or a mix of all three), this unique guide uses three different approaches to help you engage with each topic and revise in a way that suits you.

It will reinforce all the skills and concepts on the Key Stage 3 course, ensuring you are well prepared for end of key stage tests and assessments and can progress confidently on to your GCSEs.

Key Features

This guide neatly packages the KS3 course into short revision modules, each about 30 minutes long, to make planning easy.

 Striking page designs, images and diagrams help you engage with the topics.

 A hands-on revision activity for each module.

 Download the relevant track for an audio walk-through of each module.

 Simple, concise explanations for effective revision.

Keyword boxes to build vocabulary.

 Quick tests to check your understanding of each module.

Mind maps summarise the key concepts at the end of each module and show how they are linked.

 Practice questions test how well you have understood the modules. Answers are provided at the back of the book.

Letts KS3 Success Maths Workbook (ISBN 9780008299125) provides further practice.

Download the FREE audio book from lettsrevision.co.uk/ks3

CONTENTS

NUMBER

ALGEBRA

RATIO, PROPORTION AND RATES OF CHANGE

CONTENTS

GEOMETRY AND MEASURES

PROBABILITY

STATISTICS

ANSWERS

INDEX

ACKNOWLEDGEMENTS

The author and publisher are grateful to the copyright holders for permission to use quoted materials and images.

P88: ©iStockphoto.com/Mike Sonnenberg

All other images are © Shutterstock.com

Every effort has been made to trace copyright holders and obtain their permission for the use of copyright material. The author and publisher will gladly receive information enabling them to rectify any error or omission in subsequent editions. All facts are correct at time of going to press.

Published by Letts Educational
An imprint of HarperCollins*Publishers*
1 London Bridge Street
London SE1 9GF

ISBN 9780008299118

Content first published 2014
This edition published 2018

10 9 8 7 6 5 4 3 2 1

© HarperCollins*Publishers* Limited 2018

All rights reserved. No part of this publication may be reproduced, stored in a retrieval system, or transmitted, in any form or by any means, electronic, mechanical, photocopying, recording or otherwise, without the prior permission of Letts Educational.

British Library Cataloguing in Publication Data.

A CIP record of this book is available from the British Library.

Commissioning Editor: Rebecca Skinner
Author: Gillian Rich
Project Manager: Shelley Teasdale
Editorial: Gwynneth Drabble
Index: Grace Wharton
Cover Design: Sarah Duxbury
Inside Concept Design: Paul Oates
Text Design and Layout: Raspberry Creative Type
Production: Karen Nulty
Printed in Great Britain by Martins the Printers

Numbers

All **integers** and fractions can be **ordered** on a number line. These are called **rational numbers** (e.g. 4.75, $\sqrt{64}$).

All other points on the number line are called **irrational numbers** (e.g. $\sqrt{2}$, π).

Together, rational and irrational numbers make up the infinite set of **real numbers**.

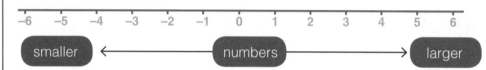

Numbers smaller than zero are called **negative** numbers.
Numbers larger than zero are called **positive** numbers.

Symbols

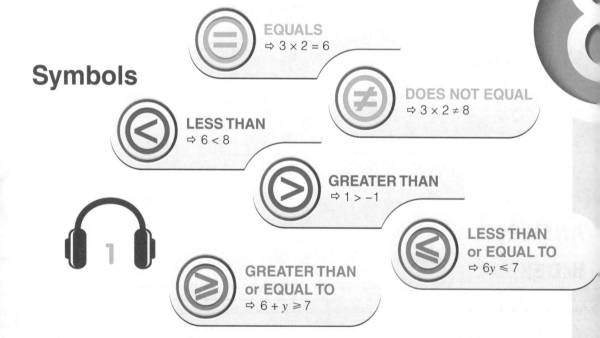

EQUALS
⇨ $3 \times 2 = 6$

DOES NOT EQUAL
⇨ $3 \times 2 \neq 8$

LESS THAN
⇨ $6 < 8$

GREATER THAN
⇨ $1 > -1$

LESS THAN or EQUAL TO
⇨ $6y \leq 7$

GREATER THAN or EQUAL TO
⇨ $6 + y \geq 7$

KEYWORDS

Integer: a positive or negative whole number or zero.
Place value: value of a digit in relation to its place within a given number.
Ordering: arranging numbers in ascending or descending value.
Decimals: a counting system based on powers of 10

MODULE 1

Decimal places

Decimals are numbers based on 10. They consist of an integer followed by a decimal point and a decimal fraction.

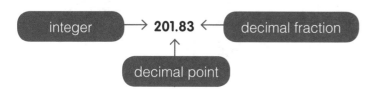

integer → **201.83** ← decimal fraction

↑ decimal point

The **place value** of each digit depends on its position relative to the **decimal point (d.p.)**.

100s	10s	1s	decimal point	$\frac{1}{10s}$	$\frac{1}{100s}$
2	0	1	•	8	3

← to next place × 10   • → to next place ÷ 10

Compare the size of these two decimal numbers by comparing each place value.

201.73   201.83

The digits are all the same except 7 < 8.

So 201.73 < 201.83

Write five different digits and a decimal point on separate pieces of paper.

Find out how many different decimal numbers can be made by arranging the pieces of paper. Choose one of the digits and write down its value in each arranged number.

1. Use one of these symbols = , ≠ , < , > , ≤ , ≥ between the following pairs of measures. Use each symbol only once.

   (i) 3kg   300g   **(ii)** 1 litre   2 pints

   (iii) 100m   1km   **(iv)** 10mm   1cm

   (v) 1 year   366 days   **(vi)** February   28 days

2. Use a number line to arrange these integers in order.

   5, 3, −1, 4, −2, 0

3. Use symbols between these pairs of decimals.

   (i) 102.4   201.1   **(ii)** 6.37   6.03

   (iii) 10.72m   107.2cm   **(iv)** 24.0567   24.0576

   (v) 0.00813   0.00803   **(vi)** 325mm   32.5cm

4. What is the value of the underlined digit?

   (i) 2<u>3</u>.4   **(ii)** 123.12<u>3</u>

   (iii) <u>4</u>20.5   **(iv)** 54.<u>6</u>

MODULE 2

KEYWORDS

Factor: a number dividing exactly into another number.

Multiple: a number that can be divided exactly by another number.

Prime number: a number that has only two factors: itself and 1.

Prime factor: a factor that is a prime number.

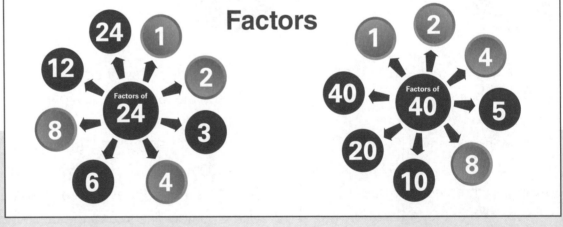

Factors

Common factors

1, 2, 4 and 8 are **common factors** of 24 and 40.

8 is the **highest common factor (HCF)** of 24 and 40.

Every number has itself and 1 as factors.

Common multiples

The **lowest** or **least common multiple (LCM)** of 2, 5 and 10 is 10.

$(2 \times 5 = 10)$ $(5 \times 2 = 10)$ $(10 \times 1 = 10)$

Multiples of a number can be found from its times table.

	1	2	3	4	5	6	7	8	9	10
1	1	2	3	4	5	6	7	8	9	10
2	2	4	6	8	10	12	14	16	18	20
3	3	6	9	12	15	18	21	24	27	30
4	4	8	12	16	20	24	28	32	36	40
5	5	10	15	20	25	30	35	40	45	50
6	6	12	18	24	30	36	42	48	54	60
7	7	14	21	28	35	42	49	56	63	70
8	8	16	24	32	40	48	56	64	72	80
9	9	18	27	36	45	54	63	72	81	90
10	10	20	30	40	50	60	70	80	90	100

multiples of 3 → 3, 6, 9, 12, 15, 18, **21**, 24, …

multiples of 7 → 7, 14, **21**, 28, 35, …

21 is the **LCM** of 3 and 7.

Draw two circles.
Write all the factors of 75 in one circle and all the factors of 120 in the other.
Put a **red** line through all the common factors and a **red** cross on the HCF.
Put a **blue** line through all the multiples of 5 and a **blue** cross on any prime factor of 75 and 120.

Prime factors

The only even **prime number** is 2. The next 10 primes are: 3, 5, 7, 11, 13, 17, 19, 23, 29, 31. You can use prime factors to find the HCF and LCM of numbers.

> Start with the smallest prime that divides exactly into the number. This is 2 if the number is even. Continue in order until 1 is reached.

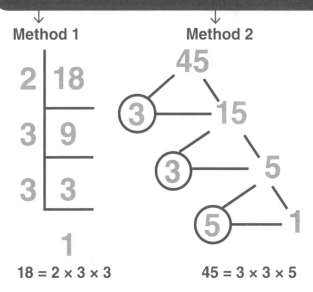

Method 1

Method 2

$18 = 2 \times 3 \times 3$ $45 = 3 \times 3 \times 5$

18 and 45 have factors 3×3 in common.
So HCF $= 3 \times 3 = 9$

To find the LCM, you only need to count the common factors once but all other factors must be included.
So LCM $= 2 \times 3 \times 3 \times 5 = 90$

1. **(i)** Find all the factors of 15 and 18.
   (ii) What is their HCF?
2. **(i)** Find the first five multiples of 9 and 36.
   (ii) What is their LCM?
3. List the primes between:
   (i) 10 and 25
   (ii) 30 and 45
4. Express the following numbers using their prime factors.
   (i) 60   **(ii)** 63

KEYWORDS

Number operations: ways of combining numbers. Remember the order using **BIDMAS: B**rackets, **I**ndices, **D**ivision, **M**ultiplication, **A**ddition, **S**ubtraction

Proper fraction: a fraction which has a denominator greater than the numerator.

Improper fraction: a fraction which has a numerator greater than the denominator.

Mixed number: a number consisting of a whole number and a fraction.

Addition [+] is inverse of subtraction [–]. Multiplication [×] is inverse of division [÷].

```
  365.4          7 ¹5 ¹4        32.5        143       165r1        21.4
+  41.8        – ₃2 ₇6 5        × 6        × 13      3)496     14)299.6
 ─────          ─────          ─────       ────      ─────      ──────
  407.2          4 8 9         195.0        429                  28↓↓
  1  1                          1 3         1430                   19↓
                                            1859                   14↓
                                            ────                   ──
                                                                   56
                                                                   56
                                                                   ──
                                                                    0
```

Always line up decimal points.

Ignore d.p. when multiplying. Replace the d.p. in the answer, counting from the right-hand side.

Working with negative numbers

Temperature in London is 12°C

Temperature in Moscow is –4°C

London is warmer than Moscow by 12 –(–4) → 16°C

Rules for multiplication and division:

Same signs (+ × +) or (– × –) → +   ← −3 × −9 = +27

Different signs (+ × –) or (– × +) → –   ← −3 × +9 = −27

Types of fractions

A fraction is part of a whole, e.g.

$\frac{2}{3}$ ← this is a **proper fraction** – the denominator (3) is greater than the numerator (2)

Changing	Improper fraction to mixed number		Mixed number to improper fraction
Rule	Divide top by bottom		Multiply whole number by bottom, add top
Examples	$\frac{13}{11} \to 1\frac{2}{11}$ $\frac{11}{6} \to 1\frac{5}{6}$	$\frac{12}{5} \to 2\frac{2}{5}$	$1\frac{1}{2} \to \frac{3}{2}$, $5\frac{1}{8} \to \frac{41}{8}$ $3\frac{2}{7} \to \frac{23}{7}$

Addition and subtraction of fractions

If the denominators are the same, just add or subtract.

$$\frac{1}{7} + \frac{5}{7} = \frac{6}{7} \qquad \frac{11}{13} - \frac{4}{13} = \frac{7}{13}$$

Otherwise, make the denominators equal by multiplying the top and bottom by the same number.

$$\frac{5}{6} + \frac{1}{4} = \frac{10}{12} + \frac{3}{12} = \frac{13}{12} \text{ or } 1\frac{1}{12}$$

multiply 5 and 6 by 2, and 1 and 4 by 3 to give the same denominator of 12

Multiplication of fractions

$$\frac{\text{Multiply numerators}}{\text{Multiply denominators}} \qquad \frac{3}{5} \times \frac{2}{7} = \frac{6}{35} \qquad \frac{6}{7^1} \times \frac{^2\cancel{14}}{25} = \frac{12}{25}$$

cancel by 7 to make numbers smaller

 Change mixed numbers to improper fractions for × and ÷

Division of fractions

Multiply after inverting the dividing fraction.

$$\frac{2}{3} \div \frac{4}{7} = \frac{^1\cancel{2}}{3} \times \frac{7}{\cancel{4}_2} = \frac{7}{6} \text{ or } 1\frac{1}{6}$$

Take two pieces of paper. Cut one piece exactly in half. Repeat, cutting one of the cut pieces in half. Cut one of the smallest pieces in half again.
Compare the size of smallest piece you have cut to your uncut piece of paper. What fraction of the original is a final piece of paper? Put together some of the pieces to make three-quarters of the original.

1. Find the answers to the following, showing all working.
   - **(i)** 905 + 89
   - **(ii)** 325 ÷ 13
   - **(iii)** 34.01 − 18.52
   - **(iv)** 214.7 × 23
   - **(v)** 753 × 14
   - **(vi)** 179.3 ÷ 11

2. Remember the signs when working out the following.
   - **(i)** −3 × +12
   - **(ii)** +20 ÷ (−4)
   - **(iii)** −3 − (−12)
   - **(iv)** −5 × −3 × −2

3. **(i)** Change $\frac{77}{45}$ to a mixed number.
   - **(ii)** Change $2\frac{5}{8}$ to an improper fraction.

4. Work out:
   - **(i)** $\frac{5}{6} + \frac{1}{4}$
   - **(ii)** $2\frac{1}{4} + 1\frac{2}{3}$
   - **(iii)** $\frac{5}{6} - \frac{4}{7}$
   - **(iv)** $3\frac{1}{3} - 1\frac{1}{5}$
   - **(v)** $1\frac{2}{5} \times 3\frac{1}{4}$
   - **(vi)** $\frac{2}{7} \div \frac{3}{4}$

KEYWORDS

Power (or index): number of times a number is multiplied by itself.

e.g. $3 \times 3 \times 3 \times 3 = 3^4$ ← power or index $\qquad y \times y = y^2$ ← power or index

↑ y squared

Roots: a square root: inverse of squaring, e.g. $2 \times 2 = 2^2 = 4$

So $\sqrt{4} = 4^{\frac{1}{2}} = 2$

↑ root shown by fractional index

b cube root: inverse of cubing, e.g. $5 \times 5 \times 5 = 5^3 = 125$

So $\sqrt[3]{125} = 125^{\frac{1}{3}} = 5$

Reciprocal: inverse of any number except zero.

reciprocal of $6 = \dfrac{1}{6}$ or 6^{-1} ← can be shown by negative index

Standard form: $A \times 10^n$, where $1 \leqslant A < 10$, is often used to show very small or very large numbers.

Standard form

EXAMPLE

$6\,200\,000 = 62 \times 100\,000$

$= 6.2 \times 10^6$

← $A \times 10^n$ →

$0.000\,000\,053\,7 = 537 \div 10^{10}$

$= 537 \times 10^{-10}$

$= 5.37 \times 10^{-8}$

Index laws

a multiplying → add **powers** to give final index

$4^2 \times 4^3 = 4^{(2+3)} = 4^5 \qquad a^2 \times a^{-3} \times a^6 = a^{(2-3+6)} = a^5$ ← normal rules apply for negative numbers

b dividing → subtract powers to give final index

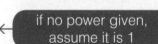

$5^7 \div 5^3 = 5^{(7-3)} = 5^4 \qquad b^9 \div b = b^{(9-1)} = b^8$ ← if no power given, assume it is 1

c raising one power to another power → multiply powers to give final index

$(3^2)^4 = 3^{(2 \times 4)} = 3^8 \qquad (c^2)^{-3} = c^{(2 \times -3)} = c^{-6}$

REMEMBER!

a Any quantity to power zero equals 1.

$7^0 = 1$ $\qquad n^0 = 1$ $\qquad 2035^0 = 1$

b If no power is given, assume it is 1.

$8 = 8^1$ $\qquad a = a^1$ $\qquad 375 = 375^1$

c A negative power gives a **reciprocal**.

$5^{-5} = \dfrac{1}{5^5}$ $\qquad p^{-3} = \dfrac{1}{p^3}$ $\qquad 20^{-6} = \dfrac{1}{20^6}$

d A fractional power gives a **root**.

$25^{\frac{1}{2}} = \sqrt{25}$ $\qquad y^{\frac{1}{3}} = \sqrt[3]{y}$ $\qquad 64^{\frac{1}{4}} = \sqrt[4]{64}$

e If asked for the value, work out to find the final answer.

$4^2 \times 4^3 = 4^{(2+3)} = 4^5 = 4 \times 4 \times 4 \times 4 \times 4 = 1024$

$(3^2)^4 = 3^{(2 \times 4)} = 3^8 = 3 \times 3 \times 3 \times 3 \times 3 \times 3 \times 3 \times 3 = 6561$

Working with numbers and letters

If there are numbers and letters in the same expression, deal with them separately,

e.g. $5x^2 \times 3x^5 = 15x^7$

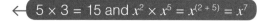 $\leftarrow$ $5 \times 3 = 15$ and $x^2 \times x^5 = x^{(2+5)} = x^7$

Write a multiplication sign, digits 1 to 9, a decimal point and several zeros on separate pieces of paper.

Arrange to make the smallest number possible. Write down this number in standard form.

Repeat with the largest number possible.

1. Write down the following in full and give the values.
   - **(i)** 5^4
   - **(ii)** 4^5
   - **(iii)** 3^6
   - **(iv)** 2^7
   - **(v)** 2^{-3}
   - **(vi)** 1^{-4}

2. Work out the value of the following.
   - **(i)** $\sqrt{36}$
   - **(ii)** $81^{\frac{1}{2}}$
   - **(iii)** $\sqrt[3]{343}$
   - **(iv)** $32^{\frac{1}{5}}$
   - **(v)** $(2^6)^{\frac{1}{2}}$
   - **(vi)** 131^0

3. Simplify the following and leave answers in index form.
   - **(i)** $y^2 \times y^3$
   - **(ii)** $a^6 \div a$
   - **(iii)** $2c \times 3c^2 \times c^4$
   - **(iv)** $4x^3 \div 2x^2$

4. Give answers to **(i)** and **(ii)** in standard form. Work out the values of **(iii)** and **(iv)**.
   - **(i)** $321\,000$
   - **(ii)** $0.000\,456$
   - **(iii)** 6.325×10^6
   - **(iv)** 1.23×10^{-7}

Decimals

- **Terminating** decimals have a finite number of digits, e.g. 0.75, 6.1
- **Recurring** decimals have digits recurring in a continuous pattern after the decimal point,

  e.g. 0.333 33..., 0.272 727 2..., 0.123 412 341 2 ...

  These can be written as $0.\dot{3}$, $0.\dot{2}\dot{7}$, $0.\dot{1}23\dot{4}$.

  The $\cdot$ above a number indicates the repeating pattern.

Percentages (%)

A percentage can be written as a **fraction** with the denominator 100. Always give a fraction in its lowest terms.

$$11\% = \frac{11}{100}$$

$$38\% = \frac{38}{100} = \frac{19}{50} \leftarrow \text{give in lowest terms}$$

a percentage → fraction

Put percentage over 100.

$$13\% = \frac{13}{100}; \quad 75\% = \frac{75}{100} = \frac{3}{4}$$

fraction → percentage

Multiply by 100 and cancel.

$$\frac{2}{5} \times 100 = 40\%$$

b fraction → decimal

Divide numerator by denominator.

$$\frac{3}{5} = 0.6$$

$$\frac{1}{3} = 0.333... = 0.\dot{3}$$

decimal → fraction

Use place value.

$$0.7 = \frac{7}{10}; \quad 0.09 = \frac{9}{100}$$

$$0.53 = \frac{5}{10} + \frac{3}{100} = \frac{50}{100} + \frac{3}{100} = \frac{53}{100}$$

$$\uparrow (\times 10)$$

$$3.5 = 3\frac{5}{10} = 3\frac{1}{2} \text{ or } \frac{7}{2}$$

c decimal → percentage

Multiply by 100.

$$0.045 = 4.5\%; \quad 0.23 = 23\%$$

percentage → decimal

Divide by 100.

$$36\% = \frac{36}{100} = 0.36; \quad 7\% = \frac{7}{100} = 0.07$$

Writing one quantity as a percentage of another quantity

Write the first quantity as the numerator and the second quantity as the denominator.

Multiply by 100.

Units must be the same.

65p as percentage of £1.25

$$\frac{65}{125} \times 100 = \frac{13}{25} \times 100 = 52\%$$

Write down any decimal (A).
Write down any fraction (B).
Work out what percentage A is of B.

Fractions

See Module 3 (page 8) for different types of fractions.

1. Change the following to percentages.
   (i) 0.54   (ii) 1.15
   (iii) $\frac{3}{5}$ (iv) $\frac{7}{20}$
2. Change the following to fractions.
   (i) 0.13   (ii) 2.75
   (iii) 15%   (iv) 16%
3. Change the following to decimals.
   (i) 32%   (ii) 95%
   (iii) $\frac{3}{8}$ (iv) $\frac{1}{9}$
4. Express the first quantity as a percentage of the second quantity.
   (i) 8cm   2m
   (ii) 30   600
   (iii) 15   240
   (iv) 30mins   5hrs

KEYWORDS

Rounding: If an approximate or estimated answer is required, numbers and measures can be rounded to an appropriate degree of accuracy (usually the same as the question).

Decimal place: If an approximate answer is required, numbers and measures can be rounded to a given number of decimal places. These are counted from the decimal point towards the right-hand side of the number.

Significant figures: If an approximate answer is required, numbers and measures can be rounded to a given number of significant figures. These are counted from first non-zero digit on the left-hand side of the number.

Rounding integers to the nearest 10, 100, 1000 or any power of 10

EXAMPLE

82 739 people attended a football match at Wembley Stadium.

Attendance to the nearest 10 → 82 740   ← 39 is nearer 40 than 30

Attendance to the nearest 100 → 82 700   ← 739 is nearer 700 than 800

Attendance to the nearest 1000 → 83 000   ← 2739 is nearer 3000 than 2000

These approximate numbers may be used if an estimate of attendance is required.

MODULE 6

Rounding integers to a given number of decimal places (d.p.)

Look at the next digit. If it is greater than or equal to (⩾) 5, add 1.

If it is less than (<) 5, ignore it.

EXAMPLES

Round 45.247 to **a** 1 d.p. **b** 2 d.p.

1st d.p.   2nd d.p.

a   45.247   → 45.2 rounded to 1 d.p.   ← 4 < 5 so ignore

3rd d.p.

b   45.247   → 45.25 rounded to 2 d.p. ← 7 > 5 so add 1 to previous digit

Rounding integers to a given number of significant figures (s.f. or sig. fig.)

EXAMPLES

Round 70 534 to **a** 1 s.f. **b** 2 s.f. **c** 3 s.f.

a 70 534   → 70 000 rounded to 1 s.f. ← 7 is the first s.f. and 4 zeros used

b 70 534   → 71 000 rounded to 2 s.f. ← 7, 1 are the 2 s.f.
$$5 \rightarrow 0 \text{ so add 1 to}$$
previous digit

c 70 534   → 70 500 rounded to 3 s.f. ← 7, 0, 5 are the 3 s.f. and
$$3 < 5 \text{ so ignore it}$$

Use zeros to retain the place value of the remaining digits.

0.000 208 → 2 is the first significant figure

Estimating answers

Round each part of a calculation to find an estimated value.

EXAMPLE

Estimate 627 divided by 26 then work out the actual answer.

Estimated: $627 \div 26 \approx 630 \div 30 = 21$

≈ means 'is approximately equal to'

Actual: $627 \div 26 = 24.12 \,(2 \text{ d.p.})$

= same order of magnitude or roughly the same size

Draw six boxes □ in a line.
Throw a dice six times, writing each number in a box.

a Round the number formed by the six digits to the nearest 10, 100, 1000.

b Round the number formed by the six digits to 3 s.f.

c Put a decimal point between the 1st and 2nd digits. Round this number to 3 d.p.

1. Round the following to the power of 10 given in brackets.
   (i)   433 (10)   **(ii)**   1061 (100)
   (iii) 2379 (1000) **(iv)**   8182 (10)

2. Round the following to the number of decimal places given in brackets.
   (i)   1076.08 (1 d.p.)
   (ii)   0.003 09 (4 d.p.)
   (iii) 73.462 35 (3 d.p.)
   (iv) 53.264 37 (4 d.p.)

3. Round the following to the number of significant figures given in brackets.
   (i)   9.347 (2 s.f.)
   (ii)   0.003 52 (1 s.f.)
   (iii) 4357 (1 s.f.)
   (iv) 84.09 (2 s.f.)

4. Calculate the floor area of a room measuring 6.67m by 4.43m.
   (i)   to 1 d.p.
   (ii)   to the nearest square metre
   (iii) to 2 d.p.

All calculators are different. It is useful to spend time getting used to a calculator and reading its instruction manual. This may have to be accessed online. The 'Shift' key may be needed to access some functions.

Calculator keys

Memory

Examples of memory keys

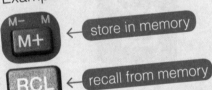 ← store in memory

RCL ← recall from memory

Brackets

← use when the order of calculation is important

Powers

reciprocals powers of 10

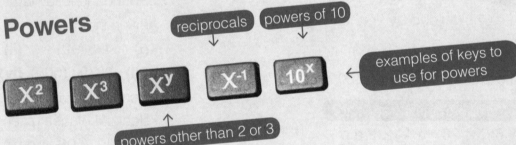

examples of keys to use for powers

↑
powers other than 2 or 3

Write down all the integers between 0 and 10.
Choose any five integers from the list to make a five-digit number.
Make a four-digit number from the remaining integers.
Use a calculator to multiply together the two numbers.
Use a calculator to divide the second number by the first.
Give the answers in standard form.

Roots

Examples of keys to use for roots

roots other than 2 or 3

Trigonometric functions

keys for trigonometrical problems using angles

use key

keys for inverse trigonometrical functions for finding angles

Fractions

useful for working with fractions

π

normally need shift key to access π for circle calculations

Exponent

EXP

use for standard form instead of 10^x

EXAMPLE

2.37×10^{12}

Enter **2 . 3 7** followed by **EXP 1 2 =** or **×10ˣ 1 2 =**

← power of 10

Calculator display may show

`2.37¹²`

---

1. Work out the following, giving your answers to 2 decimal places.
   - (i) $23.245 - 16.3$
   - (ii) 8.508×1.27
   - (iii) $15.36\text{kg} + 13.47\text{kg} + 4.603\text{kg}$
   - (iv) $4.336 \div 2$

2. Work out the following, giving your answers to 2 significant figures.
   - (i) $12^4 \times 3^7$
   - (ii) $\sqrt[3]{179} - \sqrt{39}$

3. (iii) $15^3 \div 4^2$
   (iv) $\sqrt{(8^2 - 3^2)}$

3. Use the fraction key for the following. Give your answers in their lowest terms.
   - (i) $\frac{7}{15} + \frac{5}{6}$
   - (ii) $2\frac{2}{9} + 1\frac{1}{5}$
   - (iii) $1\frac{3}{5} - \frac{9}{20}$
   - (iv) $1\frac{7}{8} \div 2\frac{1}{2}$

4. Give these answers in standard form.
   - (i) $(5.53 \times 10^2) \times (8.003 \times 10^3)$
   - (ii) $\dfrac{4.951 \times 10^2}{2 \times 10^3}$

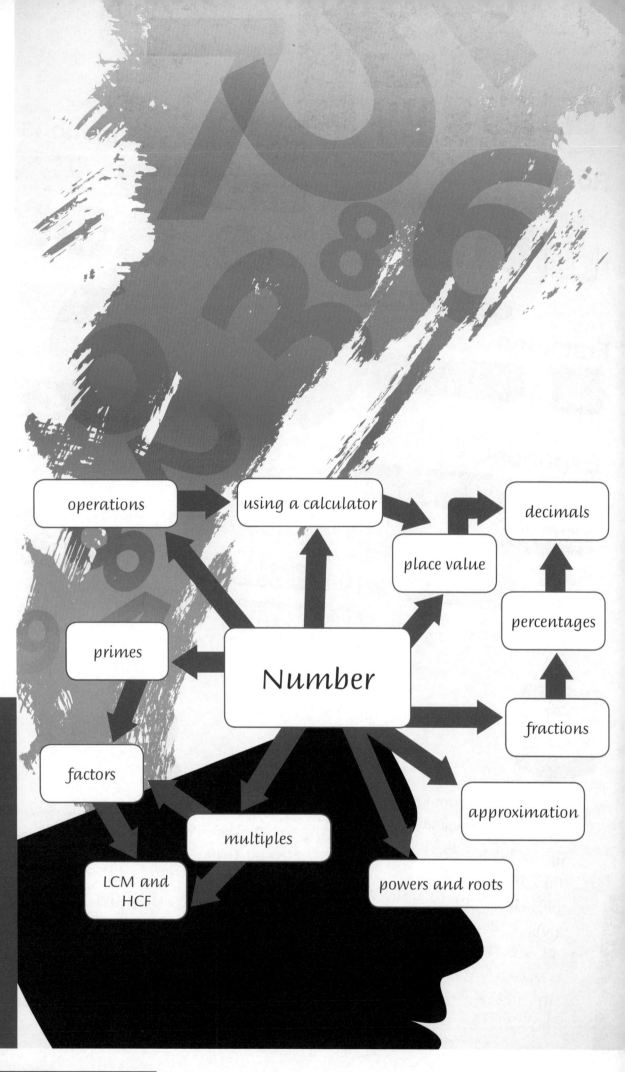

operations

using a calculator

decimals

place value

primes

Number

percentages

fractions

factors

approximation

multiples

LCM and HCF

powers and roots

1. These cards can be used once each time to make different three-digit numbers.

    a What three-digit numbers less than 650 can be made? **[1]**

    b Another card is added. They are arranged in two pairs to make two square numbers.

       What is the number on the fourth card? **[1]**

    c What are the square numbers? **[1]**

2. This diagram shows factors of 15.

    a Draw a diagram to show factors of 18. **[1]**

    b What is the HCF of 15 and 18? **[1]**

    c What is the LCM of 15 and 18? **[1]**

    d Reduce the LCM to its prime factors. **[1]**

3. Look at these five numbers:

    a Use two of these five numbers to make the largest fraction possible. **[1]**

    b Use two of these five numbers to make the smallest fraction possible. **[1]**

    c **i** Add the largest and smallest fractions that can be made.
        Give your answer as an improper fraction. **[1]**

      ii Subtract the smallest fraction from the largest fraction.
        Give your answer as a mixed number. **[1]**

     iii Multiply the largest and the smallest fractions.
        Give your answer as a percentage. **[1]**

     iv Divide the largest fraction by the smallest fraction.
        Give your answer as a decimal. **[1]**

    d Use four of these five numbers to make two equivalent fractions. **[1]**

PRACTICE QUESTIONS

KEYWORDS

Expression: a statement using letters and numbers.

$3a^2 + b + 1$

Equation: two equal statements or expressions connected by an equals sign (=).

$3 + x = 3x - 1$

8

Term: part of an expression or equation.

$2y$; $16c^2$

Coefficient: the number or letter multiplying an algebraic term.

$5ab$; $\dfrac{3d}{4}$ ← use fractions rather than decimals

Formula: an equation used to find quantities when given certain values.

$V = l \times b \times h$

Function: a relationship between dependent variables.

$f(x) = x^2 + x$

Inequality: a statement that one expression is greater than or less than another.

$x < 3$; $y > -2$

Brackets: used to show terms are treated together.

$2(a + b) = 2a + 2b$ ← Multiply each term inside brackets by the coefficient and remember signs, e.g. $-3(x - 2y) = -3x + 6y$. Signs (+ or −) are attached to the term which follows.

Write down any name of four or more letters.

Write down any non-zero number < 10 under each letter.

Use a different number for each letter.

Work out: 1st letter ÷ last letter.

Multiply together: 2nd and alternate letters.

Add together: 1st and alternate letters.

Subtract: 4th letter from 3rd letter.

Algebraic notation

In algebra, numbers are often substituted by letters.

EXAMPLES

$a \times b = ab$ ← this is also equal to $b \times a = ba$

$c + c + c = 3 \times c = 3c$ $\quad$ $p \div q = \dfrac{p}{q}$

$y \times y = y^2$ $\quad\quad$ $x \times x \times x \times y \times y = x^3y^2$

The letters are **variables** and are usually written in alphabetical order.

$t \times 3s \times 2r \times 4 = 24rst$ ← variable – a letter taking any value

Coefficients are **constants** and are written in front of the letters.

Do not write a coefficient of 1.

$1a = a$

Whole term is zero if coefficient is zero.

$0 \times a = 0$

Powers in expressions

linear expression: the highest power of the variable is 1.

quadratic expression: the highest power of the variable is 2.

1. Simplify each of the following into one term.
    (i) $x \times x \times x \times x$
    (ii) $\dfrac{y \times y \times y}{y}$
    (iii) $2 \times a \times 3 \times a \times b$
    (iv) $b \times b \times 0$

2. Simplify each of the following into one term.
    (i) $a^3 \times a^5$
    (ii) $b^6 \div b^2$
    (iii) $(c^3)^2$
    (iv) $(d^2)^{\frac{1}{2}}$

3. Simplify each of the following into one term.
    (i) $a + a + a$
    (ii) $b - 2b - c + 2c$
    (iii) $x + x + p + 3$
    (iv) $4 - y + 3y - 1$

4. Multiply out the brackets in each of the following.
    (i) $3(a + 4b)$
    (ii) $-2(2c + 3d)$
    (iii) $5(x - y + z)$
    (iv) $-3(p - q + 2r)$

Collecting like terms

To simplify an expression, collect all the terms with the same index.

EXAMPLES

$2a + 4b - a + 2c - b = a + 3b + 2c$

> these have different indices so they cannot be combined

$x^2 + 4x - y - 2y^2 + x + 2y = x^2 + 5x + y - 2y^2$

> these have different indices so they cannot be combined

$4ab + b^2 - ba + 3 = 3ab + b^2 + 3$ ← $ba = ab$

Expanding brackets

EXAMPLE

$2(y + 1) + 3y(y - 5) = 2y + 2 + 3y^2 - 15y$

> expand or multiply out brackets

$= 3y^2 - 13y + 2$ ← collect like terms

To multiply or expand the product of two brackets, each term in the first bracket multiplies each term in the second bracket. Like terms are collected,

e.g. $(x + 2)(x + 3)$
$= x^2 + 3x + 2x + 6$
$= x^2 + 5x + 6$

$x^2 + 4x - y - 2y^2$

$x^2 + 5x + y$

Write down a term using 'p'.
Write down a term using 'q'.
Put them together in brackets, using + or – between them.
Repeat, so there are two pairs of terms in brackets.
Multiply them together and simplify.

EXPRESSIONS

MODULE 9

Difference of two squares

The **difference of two squares** is an expression formed by multiplying two brackets with the same terms but different signs.

EXAMPLES

a $(a + b)(a - b) = a^2 - ab + ba - b^2$

$$= a^2 - b^2$$

b $(ax + by)(ax - by) = a^2x^2 - axby + byax - b^2y^2$

$$= a^2x^2 - b^2y^2$$

c $(3p + 2)(3p - 2) = 9p^2 - 6p + 6p - 4$

$$= 9p^2 - 4$$

d $64 - 49d^2 = (8 + 7d)(8 - 7d)$

↑ ↑

square root each term to factorise into brackets

Factorising expressions

Factorising expressions is the opposite of expanding brackets. To factorise, find a common factor and insert brackets.

$4a^2 - 12a$

$= 4(a^2 - 3a)$ ← common factor is 4

$= 4a(a - 3)$ ← common factor is a

1. Collect like terms for each of the following.
   - **(i)** $8a^2 + 5a - a^2 + 3a$
   - **(ii)** $4ab - 5ba + 7ab + a + b$
   - **(iii)** $3c^2 - 2c + c^2 + d$
   - **(iv)** $2x + x^2 - xy + y^2 - 2xy$

2. Factorise, by taking out the common factors in each of the following.
   - **(i)** $mn + 3n + n^2$
   - **(ii)** $4ab - 8b^2$
   - **(iii)** $2x^2 + 6x$
   - **(iv)** $10y - 5y^2 + 15xy$

3. Expand the brackets and simplify each of the following.
   - **(i)** $(a + 7)(a - 2)$
   - **(ii)** $(b - 1)(b + 6)$
   - **(iii)** $(3p + 2)(3p - 2)$
   - **(iv)** $(2p + 5)(2p - 5)$

4. Factorise these expressions using the difference of two squares.
   - **(i)** $q^2 - 36$
   - **(ii)** $9b^2 - 49$
   - **(iii)** $25 - 4y^2$
   - **(iv)** $81 - 121r^2$

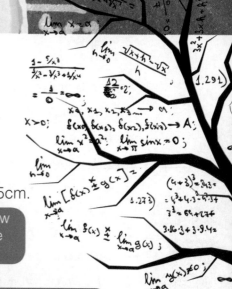

Deriving a formula

EXAMPLE

A rectangle has a length three times its width. Derive a formula to find its perimeter and area.

Let P = perimeter, A = area, l = length, w = width ← always define letters used

$P = l + w + l + w$

$\quad = 2(l + w)$

$l = 3w$, so $P = 2(3w + w)$

$\quad\quad\quad = 2 \times 4w = 8w$

$\quad\quad$ So $P = 8w$

$A = l \times w$

$l = 3w$, so $A = 3w \times w = 3w$

So $A = 3w$

Substituting into a formula

EXAMPLE

The formula for finding the area of a trapezium is
$$A = \frac{1}{2}(a + b)h$$

Calculate the area (A) if a = 6cm, b = 5cm, h = 4.5cm.

$A = \frac{1}{2}(6 + 5) \times 4.5$ ← it is sensible to show substitution before calculating

$\quad = \frac{1}{2} \times 11 \times 4.5$

$\quad = 24.75\text{cm}^2$ ← remember to give units if relevant

Changing the subject of a formula

EXAMPLES

a Make a the subject of the formula $v = u + at$

$$v = u + at$$

$$v - u = at \qquad \leftarrow \text{isolate term with } a$$

$$\frac{v - u}{t} = a \qquad \leftarrow \text{isolate } a$$

b Make r the subject of the formula $A = \pi r^2$

$$A = \pi r^2$$

$$\frac{A}{\pi} = r^2 \qquad \leftarrow \text{isolate term } r^2$$

$$\sqrt{\frac{A}{\pi}} = r \qquad \leftarrow \text{square root to find } r$$

$-12x + 10 = 3x - 7$

  🎧 10

Draw this table:

$b \downarrow \rightarrow a$	3	4	5
2			
4			
3			

Fill in each square according to $a + 2b$.

1. Work out the following.
   - **(i)** A cuboid has length twice its width and height three times its width. Write a formula for its volume (V).
   - **(ii)** Write a formula for the cost (C) of P pencils at 35p and S sharpeners at 60p each.

2. Calculate each of the following by substituting in the given values. Use $\pi = 3.142$ or the π key. Give your answers to 2 d.p.
   - **(i)** $C = 2\pi r \quad (r = 5\text{mm})$
   - **(ii)** $A = \pi r^2 \quad (r = 3.5\text{cm})$
   - **(iii)** $V = \pi r^2 h \quad (r = 2.5\text{cm}, h = 7\text{cm})$
   - **(iv)** $V = \frac{4}{3}\pi r^3 \quad (r = 3\text{cm})$

3. Change the subject of each formula to the letter in brackets after it.
   - **(i)** $P = 2(l + w) \quad (w)$
   - **(ii)** $V = \pi r^2 h \quad (h)$
   - **(iii)** $A = \frac{1}{2}bh \quad (h)$
   - **(iv)** $V = \frac{4}{3}\pi r^3 \quad (r)$

4. This is the formula for converting Celsius temperatures to Fahrenheit:
   $$F = \frac{9C}{5} + 32$$
   - **(i)** What is the Fahrenheit temperature equivalent to 28°C?
   - **(ii)** What is the Celsius temperature equivalent to 75°F?

KEYWORDS

Deriving a formula: translating a given situation or procedure into mathematical language.

Substituting into a formula: putting given values into a formula to work out a quantity.

Changing the subject of a formula: rearranging a formula to make a calculation easier.

Solving equations

Always keep both sides of an equation balanced.
Look at these examples of **linear equations**:

EXAMPLES

a $3a = 18$

$a = \dfrac{18}{3}$ ← divide both sides by 3 to isolate a

$a = 6$

b $4b + 3 = 11$

$4b = 11 - 3 = 8$ ← subtract 3 from both sides to isolate the b term

$b = \dfrac{8}{4}$ ← divide both sides by 4 to isolate b

$b = 2$

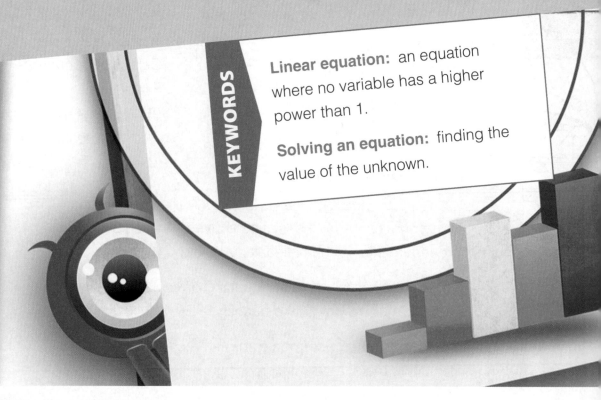

KEYWORDS

Linear equation: an equation where no variable has a higher power than 1.

Solving an equation: finding the value of the unknown.

EQUATIONS

MODULE 11

c $\quad \dfrac{2c}{5} = -6$ $\qquad\qquad\qquad$ ← multiply both sides by 5 to isolate the c term

$\quad 2c = 5 \times -6 = -30$ $\qquad\qquad$ ← divide both sides by 2 to isolate c

$\quad c = -\dfrac{30}{2}$

$\quad c = -15$

d $\quad 3d + 9 = 17 - 5d$ $\qquad\qquad$ ← add 5d to both sides, subtract 9 from both sides to separate letter and number terms

$\quad 3d + 5d = 17 - 9$

$\quad 8d = 8$

$\quad d = 1$

e $\quad 5(e - 7) = 2(e + 5)$ $\qquad\qquad$ ← expand the brackets

$\quad 5e - 35 = 2e + 10$ $\qquad\qquad$ ← add 35 to both sides, subtract 2e from both sides

$\quad 5e - 2e = 35 + 10$

$\quad 3e = 45$

$\quad e = \dfrac{45}{3} = 15$

Give a different non-zero number ⩽ 10 to each of the letters: a, b, c, d.
Use the letters to form different equations, each with one unknown.
How many equations can be made giving an answer of 20?

Solve all the following equations.

1. (i) $\quad 4x = 32$ $\qquad$ (ii) $\quad 9y = -153$
    (iii) $\quad \dfrac{2p}{3} = 1$ $\qquad$ (iv) $\quad d - 6 = 11$
    (v) $\quad 3x + 8 = 29$ $\quad$ (vi) $\quad 6f - 15 = 21$

2. (i) $\quad 3y + 4 = 2 - y$
    (ii) $\quad 4x + 7 = 25 - 2x$
    (iii) $\quad 3c - 29 = 3 - 5c$
    (iv) $\quad 4d + 15 = 8 + 5d$

3. (i) $\quad 2(3 + 2a) = 42$
    (ii) $\quad 3(b + 12) = 7(b - 4)$
    (iii) $\quad 5(c - 3) = 8(c - 6)$
    (iv) $\quad 6(d - 2) - 2(d + 4) = 8$

Plotting coordinates

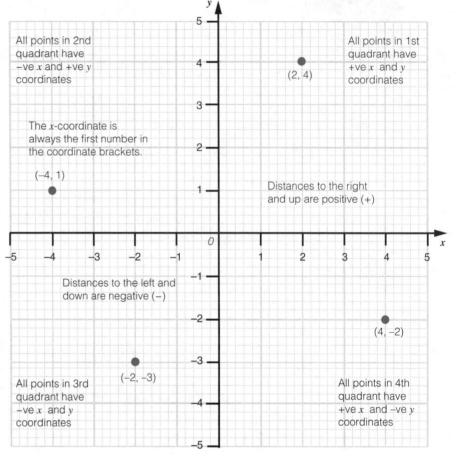

All points in 2nd quadrant have −ve x and +ve y coordinates

All points in 1st quadrant have +ve x and y coordinates

(2, 4)

The x-coordinate is always the first number in the coordinate brackets.

(−4, 1)

Distances to the right and up are positive (+)

The x-axis has the equation $y = 0$ because all points on the x-axis have y-coordinate = 0

Distances to the left and down are negative (−)

(4, −2)

(−2, −3)

All points in 3rd quadrant have −ve x and y coordinates

All points in 4th quadrant have +ve x and −ve y coordinates

The y-axis has the equation $x = 0$ because all points on the y-axis have x-coordinate = 0

Scales on **axes** x and y may be different from each other, but each axis has the same scale all the way along it. The **origin** is where the axes cross at (0, 0).

Using straight lines, draw any shape or pattern on a piece of graph paper.

The points where the lines meet are the vertices (vertices is the plural of vertex).

Label each vertex with a different letter of the alphabet.

Write down the coordinates of each vertex.

Ask another person to draw the shape by giving them your coordinates.

Is it the same shape?

Graph paper is needed for this section.

1. On graph paper:
   (i) draw an x-axis and a y-axis.
   (ii) label both axes with $-5 \leqslant x \leqslant +5$ and $-5 \leqslant y \leqslant +5$.
   (iii) draw a rectangle so that there is a vertex in each **quadrant**.
   (iv) label the rectangle PQRS and write down the coordinates for each corner of the rectangle.

2. Use a scale of 1cm to 1 unit.
   (i) Draw axes with $-4 \leqslant x \leqslant +4$ and $-4 \leqslant y \leqslant +4$.
   (ii) Plot the following points:
   A $(-2, 0.8)$
   B $(-1, 0)$
   C $(0, -3)$
   D $(3, 0)$
   E $(1, 3.6)$
   (iii) Join B to D, D to E, E to B.
   (iv) Measure BD, DE, EB.
   (v) What shape is BDE?

3. Use the points plotted in question 2.
   (i) Join A to C, C to D, D to E, E to A.
   (ii) Measure AC, CD, DE, EA.
   (iii) What is shape ACDE?

4. Use the same axes.
   (i) Plot the points   P $(-3, 3)$
   Q $(-3, -3)$ R $(1, -3)$
   (ii) Use a ruler to join the three points.
   (iii) Measure $\angle$PQR.
   (iv) What is the shape PQR?

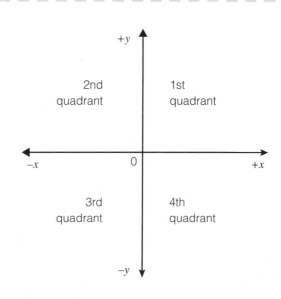

KEYWORDS

Linear function: the variable has highest power 1, e.g. $f(x) = 3x + 2$ or $y = 3x + 2$

Quadratic function: the variable has highest power 2, e.g. $f(x) = x^2 + 1$ or $y = x^2 + 1$

Cubic function: the variable has highest power 3, e.g. $f(x) = 2x^3 + x - 3$ or $y = 2x^3 + x - 3$

Reciprocal function: the variable is in the denominator of a fraction, e.g. $f(x) = \frac{1}{2x}$ or $y = \frac{1}{2x}$

Exponential function: the variable is the power (exponent) of a constant, e.g. $f(x) = 2^x$ or $y = 2^x$

Drawing graphs of functions

Calculate a table of coordinates and plot the points.

Use pencil to plot points and draw graphs in case you make errors.

a A linear function produces a straight line graph.

EXAMPLE

$y = 3x + 1$

x	−1	0	1	2
y	−2	1	4	7

Given any value of x or y, the other coordinate can be estimated by drawing lines to the graph as shown.

If necessary, the function may need changing so y is the subject,

e.g. $2y = 6x + 1$ ⟵ divide both sides by 2

$y = 3x + \frac{1}{2}$

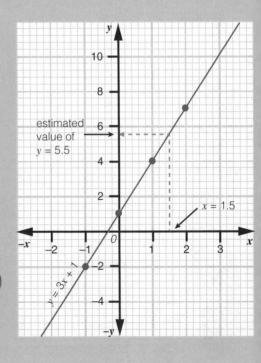

MODULE 13

Points are symmetrical as the x^2 term is always +ve.
$(+x)^2 = (-x)^2$

b Other functions produce curves. Draw a smooth curve through all the plotted points, continuing past the final points.

A **quadratic function** produces a U-shaped curve called a **parabola**,

e.g. $y = 2x^2 + 1$

x	−2	−1	0	1	2
y	9	3	1	3	9

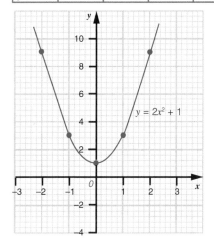

In $y = -2x^2 + 1$, the x^2 term is negative. This inverts the curve (∩).

c

Cubic function

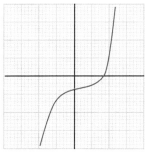

Reciprocal function

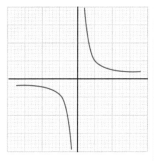

Exponential function

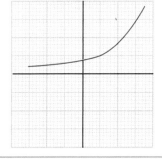

Graph paper is needed for this section.

1. Calculate a table of coordinates, plot the points and draw the graph of the function $y = 2 - 3x$.

2. Calculate a table of coordinates, plot the points and draw the graph of the function $y = 3 - x^2$.

3. Calculate a table of coordinates, plot the points and draw the graph of the function $y = x^3 + x - 2$.

4. Match the function to the correct graph below.

   (i) $f(x) = x^2 + 3$

   (ii) $f(x) = 3^x$

   (iii) $f(x) = 4x + 3$

   (iv) $f(x) = \dfrac{3}{x}$

a

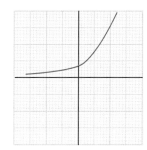

b

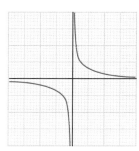

c

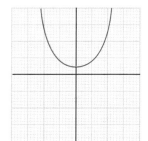

d

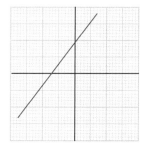

Sketch an example of a graph of each of the following types of functions.

- linear
- cubic
- exponential
- quadratic
- reciprocal

FUNCTIONS AND GRAPHS **MODULE 13** 31

Finding gradient and intercept

Compare the equation given with the general equation **($y = mx + c$)**.

e.g. $y = 2x - 1$ ← gradient = +2
y-intercept = −1

m c

Line going 'uphill' with positive gradient

Gradient = $\dfrac{\text{vertical distance}}{\text{horizontal distance}}$

$= \dfrac{4}{2} = 2$

4 units

y intercept = −1
x coord = 0

2 units

Draw x and y-axes on graph paper and label them with scales.
Draw any line going 'uphill'.
Mark any two points on the line.
Draw a right-angled triangle as shown in 'finding gradient and intercept'.
Work out the vertical and horizontal sides of triangle.
Calculate gradient from these distances.
Now repeat with a line going 'downhill'.

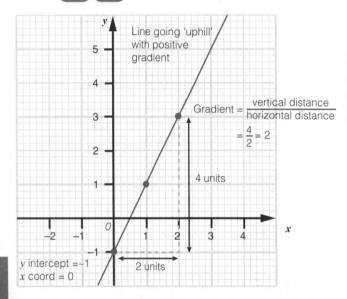

Line going 'downhill' with negative gradient

Remember: vertical distance is negative as going down.

The line gets steeper as the gradient increases.

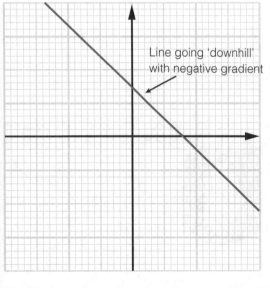

14

Finding equation of straight line

EXAMPLES

a Find the equation of a line with gradient 3 and passing through the point (0, −2).

$y = mx + c$ ← general equation

$-2 = 3 \times 0 + c$ ← substitute coordinates in the general equation

$c = -2$ ← gives value of y-intercept

Equation of line is $y = 3x - 2$

b Find the equation of a line with gradient $\frac{2}{5}$ and passing through the point (0, −1).

$y = mx + c$ ← general equation

$-1 = \frac{2}{5} \times 0 + c$ ← substitute coordinates in the general equation

$c = -1$ ← gives value of y-intercept

Equation of line is $y = \frac{2}{5}x - 1$ or $5y = 2x - 5$

↑ multiply both sides by 5 to get rid of the fraction

1. Write down the gradient and y-intercept of each of the following lines.
   - **(i)** $y = 3x + 1$
   - **(ii)** $y = 3 - 2x$
   - **(iii)** $2y = x - 4$
   - **(iv)** $5y = 3x + 10$

2. Sketch lines with the following gradients and y-intercepts.
   - **(i)** $m = 1, c = 2$
   - **(ii)** $m = -2, c = 1$
   - **(iii)** $m = 3, c = -2$
   - **(iv)** $m = -2, c = -1$
   - **(v)** Comment on lines **(ii)** and **(iv)**.

3. Calculate a table of coordinates and draw the graph of $y = 2 - x$. By drawing the vertical and horizontal distances, work out the gradient.
   Write down the y-intercept.

4. Work out the equations of the following lines.
   - **(i)** gradient = +2, passes through (0, 4)
   - **(ii)** gradient = $-\frac{1}{2}$, passes through (0, 3)
   - **(iii)** gradient = +3, passes through (1, 4)
   - **(iv)** gradient = $+\frac{3}{4}$, passes through (−2, 2)

SIMULTANEOUS EQUATIONS

Solving simultaneous equations

The solutions of a pair of simultaneous equations can be found by drawing the graphs of the equations.

The solutions are given by the coordinates of the intersection.

EXAMPLES

a Solve $\left.\begin{array}{l} y = 7 - 4x \\ 2y = 3x - 9 \end{array}\right\}$ for x and y.

First work out tables of coordinates for each equation.

$y = 7 - 4x$

x	−1	0	1
y	11	7	3

$2y = 3x - 9$

x	−1	0	1
y	−6	−4.5	−3

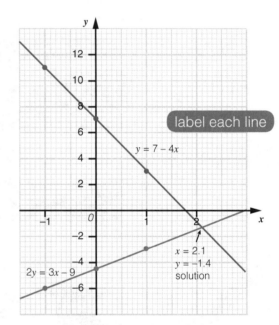

label each line

$y = 7 - 4x$

$2y = 3x - 9$

$x = 2.1$
$y = -1.4$
solution

Simultaneous equations: two equations having the same solutions or satisfied by the same pair of values,

e.g. $\left.\begin{array}{l} y = x + 2 \\ y = 8 - x \end{array}\right\}$ are both satisfied by $x = 3$, $y = 5$.

Two unknowns are involved, so two equations are needed to find x and y.

b Solving a linear equation and a quadratic equation.

A quadratic equation has two solutions for x.

Solve $\left.\begin{array}{l} y = x^2 - x - 1 \\ \\ y = x + 2 \end{array}\right\}$ for x and y.

The curve and straight line are both drawn and labelled.

The line crosses the curve twice. The coordinates of the two intersections give both solutions:

$x = -1$, $y = 1$ and $x = 3$, $y = 5$.

The coordinates of the two points where the curve crosses the x-axis ($y = 0$) give the solutions of the quadratic equation: $x = -0.6$ and $x = 1.6$

$y = x^2 - x - 1$

x	-2	-1	0	1	2	3	0.5
y	5	1	-1	-1	1	5	-1.25

The coordinates of the minimum point will help with drawing the curve.

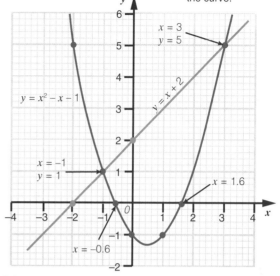

Graph paper is needed for this section.
Draw the graph of $y = x^2$ from $-4 \leqslant x \leqslant +4$
Draw a dotted straight line to the curve from $x = 2.5$
What information does this give?
Draw a dotted straight line to the curve from $y = 12$.
What information does this give?

Graph paper is needed for this section.

1. (i) Work out a table of coordinates for these two linear equations.
$$\left.\begin{array}{l} 4x + 3y = 5 \\ 5x - y = 11 \end{array}\right\}$$
   (ii) Draw the lines and label them.
   (iii) Solve the equations for x and y.

2. (i) Draw the curve for $y = -2x^2$
   (ii) On the same axes, draw the line
        $y + 10 = -2x$
   (iii) Write down the coordinates of the intersections of these graphs.

3. (i) Draw the curve for $y = x^2 - 4$
   (ii) Solve the equation $x^2 - 4 = 0$ by writing down the x-coordinates of the points on the curve where $y = 0$.

4. (i) On the same axes as in question 3, draw the curve $y = 4 - x^2$
   (ii) How does this curve relate to that in question 3?

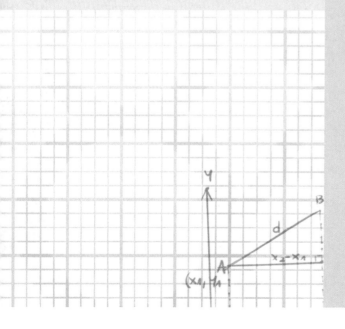

PROBLEMS AND GRAPHS

EXAMPLES

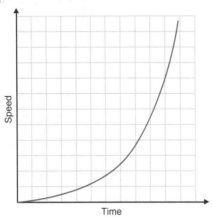

A marathon runner starts running and picks up speed.

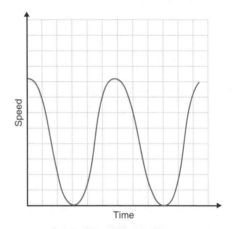

She stops and starts a couple of times.

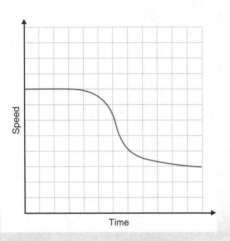

She gets tired and slows down.

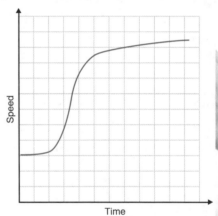

She wants to finish, so increases speed. She sprints to the end.

b A ball is thrown into the air.

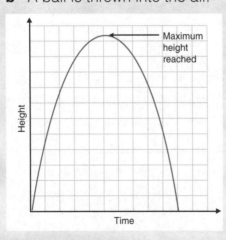

c Rainfall over a 5-hour period.

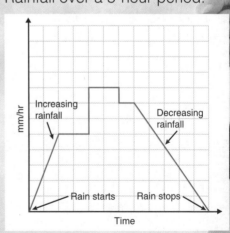

16

MODULE 16

d Showing a journey on a graph.

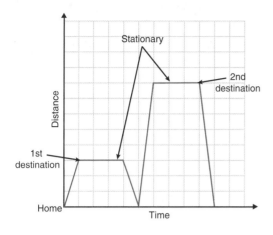

The steeper the gradient, the faster the speed.

Pick three different-shaped containers.
Pour water into each container.
Measure the depth every two seconds.
Sketch three separate graphs showing the increase of depth with time.
(vertical axis → depth, horizontal axis → time)

1. This graph illustrates a stone being thrown up into the air.

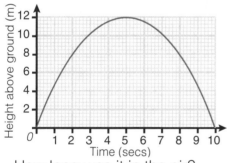

(i) How long was it in the air?

(ii) How high was the stone after 2.5secs?

(iii) How high did the stone reach?

(iv) When was the stone at 10m?

2. This graph illustrates a bus journey.

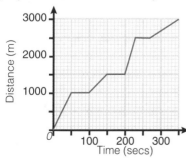

(i) How many times does the bus stop?

(ii) When is the bus travelling fastest?

(iii) How far from the start of the journey is the first stop?

(iv) How long does it stay at the 3rd stop?

3. This table shows the exterior angle (y) of a regular polygon with x sides.

x **sides**	3	4	5	6	8	10	12	15
Angle y	120°	90°	72°		45°	36°		24°

(i) Draw the curve illustrating this information.

(ii) Draw lines to the curve to find the exterior angle for a 6-sided and for a 12-sided polygon.

(iii) A regular polygon has an exterior angle of 40°.
Draw lines to the curve to find the number of sides of this polygon.

Generating sequences

EXAMPLES

a **Arithmetic sequence**: Add or subtract the same number (common difference),

e.g. Find the next two terms in these sequences.

1, 4, 7, 10, **13**, **16**, …

+3 +3 +3

> next two terms found by adding 3 each time

b **Geometric sequence**: Multiply (or divide) by the same number (common ratio).

3, 6, 12, 24, **48**, **96**, …

×2 ×2 ×2

> next two terms found by multiplying by 2 each time

c Special numbers,

e.g. square numbers → 1, 4, 9, 16, 25, …

> $1^2, 2^2, 3^2, 4^2, 5^2, …$

cubed numbers → 1, 8, 27, 64, 125, …

> $1^3, 2^3, 3^3, 4^3, 5^3, …$

primes → 2, 3, 5, 7, 11, 13, 17, …

> 1 not included as it is a factor of all prime numbers

nth term

a Generating a sequence from the nth term.

nth term $= 3n + 2$

sequence: 5   8   11,…

> substitute position number of term into nth term formula

$n = 1$ $n = 2$ $n = 3$

1st term   2nd term   3rd term

b Finding the nth term of a sequence.

2	6	10	14	…	→ look for a pattern
1st	2nd	3rd	4th	nth	→ term number
↑	↑	↑	↑	↑	
$(4 \times 1) - 2$	$(4 \times 2) - 2$	$(4 \times 3) - 2$	$(4 \times 4) - 2$	$4n - 2$	→ 4 × term no. − 2

Test the nth term by substituting $n = 5$ to find the 5th term:

$4(5) - 2 = 20 - 2 = 18$ which is the 5th term.

It is possible to find any term in a sequence using the formula for the nth term.

SEQUENCES

MODULE 17

a Make a square with four paper clips. (1 × 1)

b Add four more paper clips to make a larger square. (2 × 2)

c Repeat to make a bigger (3 × 3) square.

d Complete a table for squares with sides measuring from 1 to 10.

No. of paper clips on each side	1	2	3	4	5	→ 10
Size of square formed	1 × 1	2 × 2	3 × 3	4 × 4	5 × 5	
Total no. of paper clips	4					

e Work out a pattern to find the nth term formula.

1. Find the next two terms in these sequences.
   (i) 24, 22, 20, 18
   (ii) 11, 22, 33, 44
   (iii) 3, 9, 27, 81
   (iv) 48, 24, 12, 6

2. Find the 15th term using the nth term formula.
   (i) $2n$
   (ii) $3n + 1$
   (iii) $\dfrac{5n + 1}{2}$
   (iv) $2n^2$

3. Find the nth term of these sequences.
   (i) 2, 5, 10, 17, 26, …
   (ii) 10, 15, 20, 25, 30, …
   (iii) 0, 7, 26, 63, …
   (iv) 24, 22, 20, 18, …

4. Find the next three terms of each sequence in question 3.

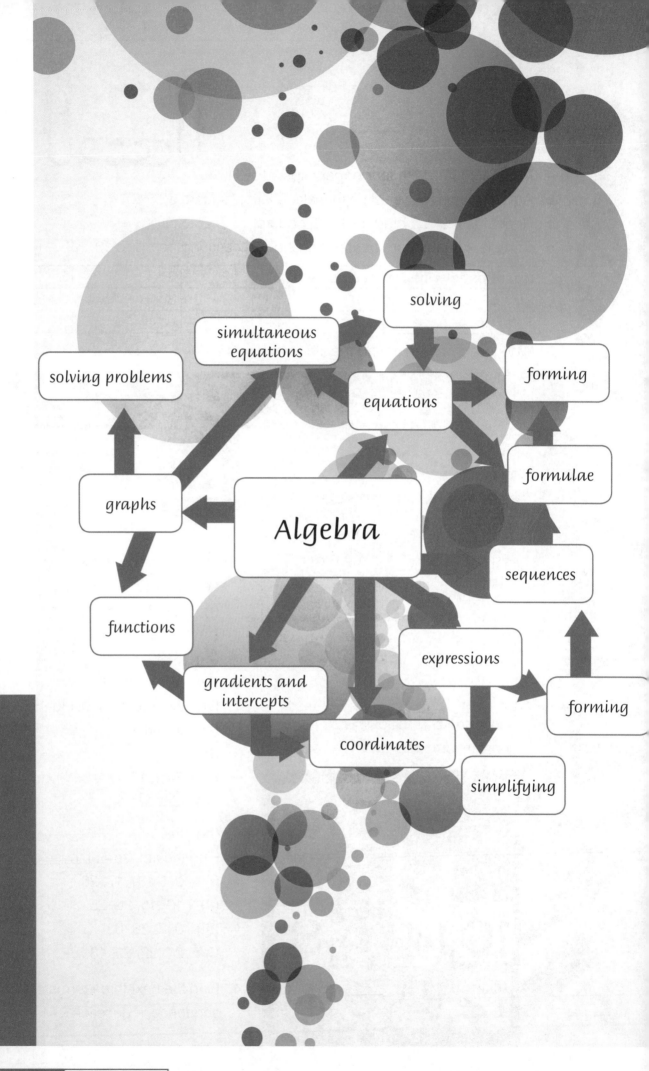

solving

simultaneous equations

solving problems

forming

equations

graphs

formulae

Algebra

sequences

functions

expressions

gradients and intercepts

forming

coordinates

simplifying

1. $p + q = 12$ $p - q = 4$

   a Write down the values of p and q to make both equations true. **[2]**

   b i Write down the left-hand side of each equation in brackets and multiply the brackets together. **[1]**

   ii What is the value of this expression if $p = 5$ and $q = 1.2$? **[1]**

2. Each point on the straight line graph $x + y = 14$ has x-coordinates and y-coordinates that add up to 14.

   a Draw the straight line $x + y = 14$. **[1]**

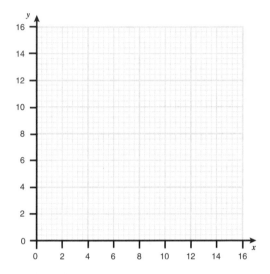

   b Write down the gradient of this line. **[1]**

   c Work out the gradient of a line $x + y = n$ where n is any integer. **[1]**

3. A triangle is made from three straws. Two more straws are added to make two triangles.

   a Copy and complete this table. **[3]**

No. of triangles	1	2	3	4	5
No. of straws	3	5			

   b What is the rule for finding the next term in this sequence? **[1]**

   c Write down the general rule for finding the number of straws needed for making n triangles, where n is any positive integer. **[1]**

PRACTICE QUESTIONS

Metric ← → metric conversion

Convert from one metric unit to another by multiplying or dividing by powers of 10.

$1cm^3 = 1ml$

kilo- → 1000
centi- → 100
milli- → $\frac{1}{1000}$

EXAMPLES

a Change 1.325kg to g.

$1.325kg = 1.325 \times 1000g$

$= 1325g$

b Change 25 000cm² to m².

$25\,000cm^2 = 25\,000 \div 10\,000 m^2$

$= 2.5m^2$

$1m^2 = 100cm \times 100cm$

c Change 356cl to litres.

$356cl = 356 \div 100 l$

$= 3.56$ litres

Learn

10 millimetres (mm) = 1 centimetre (cm)

100 centimetres = 1 metre (m)

1000 metres = 1 kilometre (km)

1 hectare (ha) = 10 000 square metres (m²)

1000 milligrams (mg) = 1 gram (g)

1000 grams = 1 kilogram (kg)

1000 kilograms = 1 tonne (t)

1000 millilitres (ml) = 1 litre (l)

100 centilitres (cl) = 1 litre (l)

Metric ← → imperial conversion

18

It is useful to learn the following conversions.

Length	Area	Volume	Mass/Weight
8km ≈ 5 miles	1 hectare (ha) ≈ 2.5 acres	1 litre ≈ 1.75 pints (pts)	1kg ≈ 2.2 pounds (lbs)
2.5cm ≈ 1 inch (in)		4.5 litres ≈ 1 gallon (gal)	450g ≈ 1lb
30cm ≈ 1 foot (ft)			28g ≈ 1 ounce (oz)
1m ≈ 1 yard (yd) = 3ft			different spellings → 1 tonne ≈ 1 ton

KEYWORDS

Metric units: measurements based on 10, e.g. millimetres, centimetres, metres.

Imperial units: previous system of measurement, some of which is still used, e.g. pints, feet, miles.

MODULE 18

CONVERTING MEASUREMENTS

Imperial units

12ins = 1ft   3ft = 1yd   8pts = 1gal   16oz = 1lb

Time conversion

Time can be measured in two forms.

EXAMPLES

a 12hr clock: two periods of 12 hours
am (before 12 noon)   pm (after 12 noon)
e.g. 6:15am   5:45pm

b 24hr clock: continuous period of 24 hours
e.g. 08:25 ← = 8:25am in 12hr clock time – 24hr clock does not use am or pm; give 4 figures, using zeros if necessary

15:55 ← = 3:55pm in 12hr clock time – subtract 12 from hour from 13:00 (1pm) and remember to add 'pm'

Compound units

Compound units are given as a ratio of two other units,

e.g. speed = $\dfrac{\text{distance}}{\text{time}}$ density = $\dfrac{\text{mass}}{\text{volume}}$

average speed = $\dfrac{\text{total distance}}{\text{total time}}$

Use a calendar or diary to find out:
a the number of days in each month.
b the number of days in a year. If it is a leap year, there will be a different answer to both **a** and **b**.
Look up 'leap year' and write down the definition.

Use the approximate conversions given on page 42 where necessary.

1. Convert the following measurements to the unit in brackets. Give answers to an appropriate degree of accuracy.
    (i)   2.64km (m)
    (ii)   1562cm (m)
    (iii) 4yds (m)
    (iv) 43km (miles)

2. Convert the following measurements to the unit in brackets. Give answers to an appropriate degree of accuracy.
    (i)   20 000m² (ha)
    (ii)   3.5pts (*l*)
    (iii) 6.53*l* (ml)
    (iv) 23gals (*l*)

3. Convert the following measurements to the unit in brackets. Give answers to 2 d.p.
    (i)   1325mg (g)
    (ii)   3.2 tonnes (kg)
    (iii) 4.5lbs (kg)
    (iv) 340g (oz)

4. (i)   How many minutes are in a day?
    (ii)   What percentage of a day is one hour? Give your answer to 3 s.f.
    (iii) How long is a TV programme starting at 6:55pm and finishing at 7:45pm?
    (iv) Convert 5:07am to 24hr clock and 23:30 to 12hr clock.

Scale drawing

Any length can be drawn to scale to enable a diagram to be displayed on a page.

EXAMPLES

a Using a **scale factor** of 1 : 20, draw a line to represent 36cm.

Length of line = 36cm ÷ 20 = 1.8cm ← to be drawn

scale factor ↑

↑ *original*

b A line measuring 10.4cm has been drawn using a scale factor of 1 : 25. What was the original distance?

original ↓

Multiply by scale factor → 10.4 × 25 = 260cm = 2.6m ← original ÷ 100

↑ *drawn line*

Map distances

Two towns E and H are 32km apart.

A map is drawn to a scale 1 : 1 000 000. What is the map distance?

32km × 1000 = 32 000m → 32 000 × 100cm = 3 200 000cm

↑ change actual distance to cm

Map distance = 3 200 000 ÷ 1 000 000 = 3.2cm ← drawn distance

↑ *scale factor*

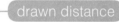

Look at a map of your local area. Measure the distance from your home to your school on the map. Check the scale on the map and convert the map distance to the actual distance.

Write down the grid reference of your home and school.

KEYWORDS

Scale: maps are drawn to scale 1 : n, where n is the distance in cm represented by 1cm on the map.

Grid reference: the coordinates of a position on a map.

Scale factor: ratio of the enlarged distance to the corresponding original distance.

Grid references

The coordinates of a point on a map are usually given using letters and numbers.

The grid reference of the Round Pond is E2.

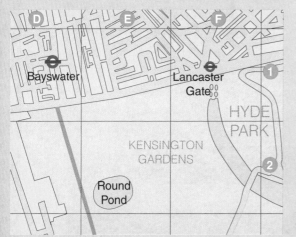

⊖ indicates a London underground station.

Compass points and bearings

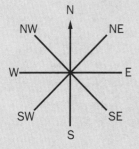

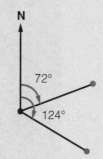

Bearings are always measured in a clockwise direction from North.

Give a bearing as a three-figure angle, e.g. 072°, 124°, 208°, 350°.

1. What length should the following lines be drawn if you are using a scale factor of 1 : 20?
   (i) 2.5m (ii) 1.36m
   (iii) 48cm (iv) 3200mm

2. What are the actual distances using a scale factor of 1 : 150 000?
   (i) 3.4cm (ii) 0.53cm
   (iii) 7.58cm (iv) 1.36cm

3. Using the map opposite, give the grid references for underground stations:
   (i) Lancaster Gate
   (ii) Bayswater

4. What is the bearing of S from T in each of these diagrams?

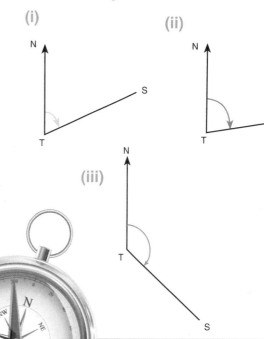

Comparing quantities using fractions

Read the question carefully to decide which quantity is the numerator and which is the denominator.

Both parts must be in the same units.

 **20**

EXAMPLES

a What fraction of a day is 45mins?

$45\text{mins} = \dfrac{3}{4} \text{ hr}$ ← numerator ← denominator   1 day = 24hrs

$\text{Fraction} = \dfrac{\left(\dfrac{3}{4}\right)}{24} = \dfrac{3}{4 \times 24} = \dfrac{1}{32}$ ← keep as fraction as required by the question

So 45 mins is $\dfrac{1}{32}$ of one day ← answer given in terms of question

b What fraction is £1.75 of £10?

$£1.75 = £1\dfrac{3}{4}$ ← express as a fraction

mixed number   improper fraction

$\text{Fraction} = \dfrac{\left(1\dfrac{3}{4}\right)}{10} = \dfrac{\left(\dfrac{7}{4}\right)}{10} = \dfrac{7}{4 \times 10} = \dfrac{7}{40}$ ← keep as fraction as required by the question

So £1.75 is $\dfrac{7}{40}$ of £10. ← answer given in terms of question

Get some counters of two different colours, A and B, so that there are more B than A. What fraction is A of the total number of counters?

What percentage is B of the total number of counters?

Add more counters of colour C. What fraction is C of the total number of counters?

What percentage is A + B of the total number of counters?

MODULE 20

COMPARING QUANTITIES

Comparing quantities using percentages

EXAMPLE

What percentage is 150cm of 4m?

First form a fraction as on page 46. $\dfrac{150cm}{4m}$

Make sure the units are the same.

Either $\dfrac{150cm}{400cm}$ or $\dfrac{1.5m}{4m}$ or $\dfrac{1\frac{1}{2}m}{4m}$

Multiply by 100 to change the fraction to a percentage.

Either $\dfrac{150 \times 100}{400}$ or $\dfrac{1.5 \times 100}{4}$ or $\dfrac{3 \times 100}{2 \times 4}$ ← units not needed once they are the same

$= 37.5\%$

1. What fraction of the first quantity is the second?
   - (i) £5   60p
   - (ii) 40km   3m
   - (iii) 6kg   7500g
   - (iv) 3 litres   250ml

2. What percentage of the first quantity is the second? Give your answer to 2 d.p. where necessary.
   - (i) 2m   25mm
   - (ii) £6.50   75p
   - (iii) 22kg   850g
   - (iv) 3000ml   4.5 litres

3. A school has 980 pupils. 425 pupils are girls.
   - (i) What fraction of the total pupils are girls?
   - (ii) Out of the total of 64 staff, 33 are men. What fraction of staff are women?
   - (iii) Counting staff and pupils together, what fraction of the whole school are male?

4. During a holiday of 12 days, a family goes to the beach on 7 days. What percentage of the holiday was not spent on the beach? Give the answer to 1 d.p.

Simplifying ratios

Ratios can be simplified in the same way as fractions. Cancel using common factors.

Make sure all parts are in the same units.

EXAMPLE

A bag contains 4 red counters and 6 green counters.

Ratio of red to green	$= 4 : 6$
	$= 2 : 3$ ← cancel by common factor 2

8 blue counters are added.

Ratio of red to green to blue	$= 4 : 6 : 8$
	$= 2 : 3 : 4$ ← cancel by common factor 2

Always give the ratio in the same order as in the question.

Dividing a quantity in a given ratio

EXAMPLE

Divide 240 in the ratio 5 : 3

Total number of ratio parts	$= 5 + 3 = 8$	← add all parts of the ratio
Single share	$= 240 \div 8 = 30$	← divide quantity by total
So 240 divided in the ratio 5 : 3 $= (5 \times 30) : (3 \times 30)$	←	multiply single share by each part of the ratio
	$= 150 : 90$	↑ **unitary method**

KEYWORDS

Ratio: compares quantities in the form $a : b$.

Unitary method: finding one unit then multiplying it by the number needed.

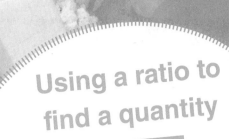

Using a ratio to find a quantity

EXAMPLE

Shortcrust pastry is made from fat and flour in the ratio 1 : 2.

How much flour is needed to make 600g pastry?

Total number of parts = 1 + 2 = 3

Single share = 600g ÷ 3 = 200g

So amount of flour = 2 × 200g
= 400g

1. Simplify these ratios to lowest terms.
   (i)   24 : 108
   (ii)   13 : 52 : 117
   (iii)   3.5l : 250ml
   (iv)   2hrs : 50mins : 300secs

2. Divide each quantity in the ratio shown.
   (i)   £360 in the ratio 3 : 5
   (ii)   24hrs in the ratio 1 : 3 : 4
   (iii)   60cm in the ratio 5 : 12 : 13
   (iv)   280km in the ratio 7 : 4 : 3

3. Three grandchildren are left £33 000 in the ratio 2 : 5 : 4.
   How much does each grandchild receive?

4. Green paint is made by mixing 3 parts yellow paint to 2 parts blue paint.
   If there is 80ml of blue paint and 140ml of yellow paint, what is the maximum quantity of green paint that can be made?

Get some counters of three different colours, A, B, C, so that B > A > C.
Write down the ratio of:
A : B : C
A : B + C
A + B : C

Percentage change

To find percentage change:

Method 1	Method 2
Multiply the original amount by a multiplier.	Calculate the percentage increase or decrease. Add this to / subtract it from the original amount.

a Increase: multiply by (1 + % as decimal)

e.g. The number of people visiting a museum in March was 8300. There was an increase of 15% in April.

How many visitors were there in April?

Method 1

Visitors in April = 8300 × (1 + 0.15)

= 8300 × 1.15

= 9545

Method 2

Use 15% = 0.15 or $\frac{15}{100}$ in calculation.

Extra visitors = 15% of 8300

= 0.15 × 8300 = 1245

Total visitors in April = 8300 + 1245

= 9545

b Decrease: multiply by (1 − % as decimal)

e.g. A TV costing £880 is discounted by 10%. What is the sale price?

Method 1

10% = 0.1 as decimal

Sale price = £880 × (1 − 0.1)

= £880 × 0.9

= £792

Method 2

Decrease = 10% of £880 = 0.1 × £880

= £88

Sale price = £880 − £88

= £792

KEYWORDS

Percentage increase: percentage by which a quantity gets larger – also called gain, profit.

Percentage decrease: percentage by which a quantity gets smaller – also called reduction, discount, less.

Interest: amount of money paid on savings or loans.

Original value ← divide amount by multiplier

EXAMPLE

A coat costs £85 in a sale. It has been discounted by 20%. What is its original price?

Original price = £85 ÷ (1 − 0.2) = £85 ÷ 0.8
= £106.25

> 20% = 0.2 as a decimal

Simple interest ← paid annually (every year)

Simple interest = invested amount × period of investment (yrs) × rate of interest per year (decimal)

e.g. Find the simple interest on £1800 invested for 3 years at a rate of 2.5% per year.

> amount

> rate

Simple interest = £1800 × 3 × 0.025 = £135

> time period

1. (i) My gas bill is usually £786. It is to be increased by 5%. How much is the new bill?

   (ii) A normal bag of apples contains 8 apples. A special bag contains 25% free. How many apples are in the special offer bag?

2. (i) A washing machine costing £425 is discounted by 15% in a sale. What is the sale price?

   (ii) The price of a holiday is £570 per adult. The price for a child under 12 is discounted by 12%. How much is paid for a child?

3. A salary is £2916 per month after a 3% salary rise. What is the salary before the rise?

4. An amount of £750 is invested in a savings account at a simple interest rate of 2.7% per year. How much will be in the account after:

   (i) 2 years?

   (ii) $3\frac{1}{2}$ years?

Take a handful of counters.
Count them.
Increase the amount by 20%.
If the new amount is the result of a reduction of 5%, what was the original amount?

Direct proportion

EXAMPLES

The cost of fuel to a motorist is directly proportional to the number of litres he puts into his car's petrol tank.

a Petrol costs £1.32 per litre
So 15 litres will cost 15 × £1.32 = £19.80

b Below are the basic ingredients for making tomato soup for 4 people.
What quantities of ingredients are needed to make tomato soup for 12 people?

Method 1: 12 ÷ 4 = 3 so 3 times as much is needed. Multiply each quantity by 3 to find quantities for 12.

Method 2: First work out how much is needed for 1 person, then multiply by 12.

for 4	÷ 4 = for 1	× 12 = for 12	unitary method
400g tomatoes	100g	1200g (1.2kg)	
2 onions	0.5	6	
80g butter	20g	240g	
600ml stock	150ml	1800ml (1.8*l*)	

23

Draw two axes.

Label the vertical axis
→ °F (0 ⩽ °F ⩽ 220)

Label the horizontal axis
→ °C (0 ⩽ °C ⩽ 120)

Using 0°C = 32°F and 100°C = 212°F, draw a graph to convert temperatures between the scales.

Choose different temperatures in each scale and find the equivalent temperatures in the other scale.

TIP
Draw a dotted line from the chosen temperature to the conversion line, then a dotted line to the other scale.

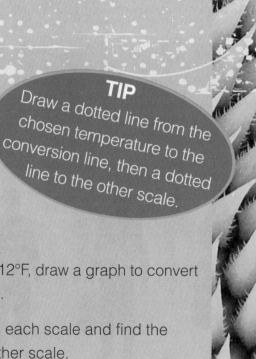

Using graphs for direct proportion

If two quantities increase in direct proportion to each other, a straight-line graph can be used to convert from one to the other,
e.g. converting euros (€) to £.

Use zero € = zero £ and this exchange rate to draw a graph.
€1.18 = £1   €1 = 85p

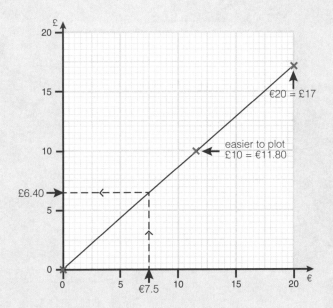

Inverse proportion

EXAMPLE

A house is being painted in 5 days by 3 decorators. How long would it take if 4 decorators were working at the same rate?

3 decorators take 5 days
So 1 decorator takes 5 × 3 = 15 days ← *longer time, so multiply*

4 decorators will take 15 ÷ 4 = $3\frac{3}{4}$ days ← *shorter time as more decorators*

1. A car is driven 290 miles in 5 hours of steady driving.
   (i) How far could it be driven in 7 hours?
   (ii) How long would it take to drive 200 miles?
2. A pear crumble for 4 people uses 250g flour, 128g sugar, 128g margarine, 450g pears. Work out the ingredients needed for:
   (i) 6 people
   (ii) 8 people
3. A minibus is hired by 8 people. They each pay £14.50. The minibus seats 10 people.
   How much would each person have had to pay if the minibus had been full?
4. This week £1 will buy $1.62. On graph paper, draw a graph to convert £ and $. What are the missing amounts?
   (i) £350 = $ ☐
   (ii) £500 = $ ☐
   (iii) $500 = £ ☐
   (iv) $350 = £ ☐

Proportion: amounts are in proportion if they increase or decrease in the same ratio.

Direct proportion: amounts are in direct proportion if they increase in the same ratio.

Inverse proportion: amounts are in inverse proportion if one increases as the other decreases in the same ratio.

KEYWORDS

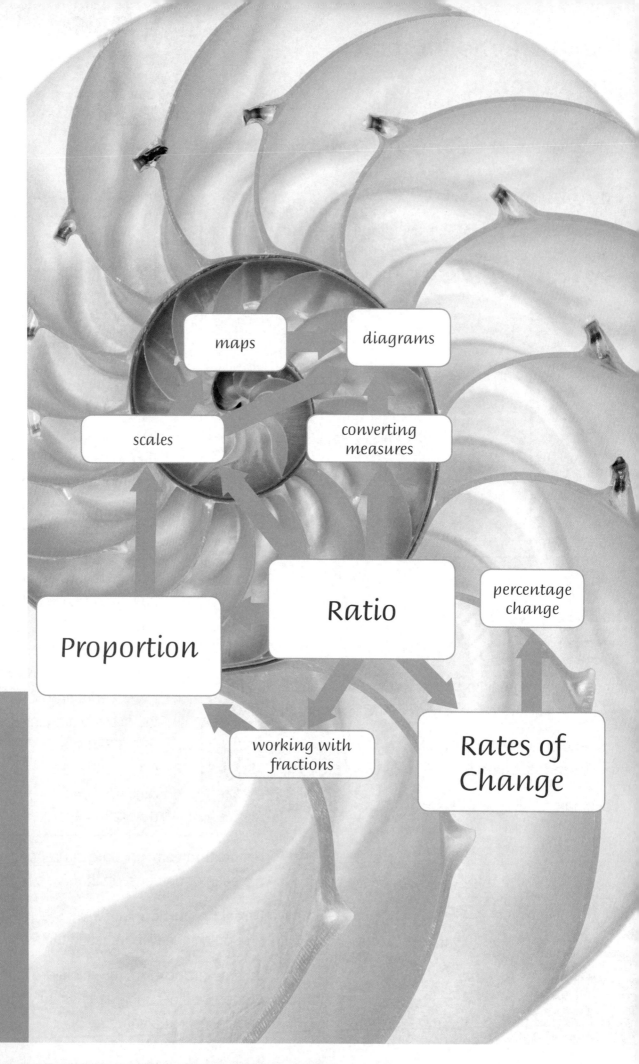

maps

diagrams

scales

converting measures

Proportion

Ratio

percentage change

working with fractions

Rates of Change

1. A jumper is knitted using 12 balls of colour A, 2 balls of colour B and 1 ball of colour C.

   Each ball contains 60% wool and 40% acrylic, weighs 50g and costs £4.50.

   a How much does the jumper weigh in kg? **[1]**

   b What is the ratio of wool to acrylic? Give the ratio in its simplest terms. **[1]**

   c The cost of a 50g ball of wool increases by 5%.

   What will it cost now to buy all the wool for the jumper? **[1]**

   d A similar jumper costs £65 to buy in a shop. Suggest reasons for choosing each of the jumpers. **[2]**

2. A road atlas uses a scale of 1 : 158 400

   The distance from Sheffield to Leeds is 33 miles.

   a What is this distance in kilometres? **[1]**

   b What distance would this be on the map? **[1]**

   c Sheffield is on a bearing of 170° from Leeds. Draw a sketch to illustrate this bearing. **[1]**

3. These are the ingredients used to make a litre of fruit drink.

$\frac{1}{2}$ litre apple juice	$\frac{3}{10}$ litre orange juice	$\frac{1}{5}$ litre mango juice

   a Work out the percentage of each fruit juice in the fruit drink. **[3]**

   b If $2\frac{1}{2}$ litres of fruit drink are required, what quantities of ingredients are needed? **[3]**

   c Write down the ratio of the fruit drink ingredients in its simplest terms. **[1]**

Perimeter

The perimeter of any 2D shape is found by adding all the sides of the shape.

EXAMPLE

Perimeter (P) of a rectangle $= l + w + l + w = 2(l + w)$

$$P = 2(6.5 + 3) = 2 \times 9.5\text{cm}$$

make sure all units are the same

$$= 19\text{cm}$$

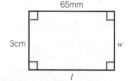

Area

EXAMPLE

Area (A) of a rectangle $= l \times w = lw$

$$A = 65\text{mm} \times 3\text{cm} = 6.5\text{cm} \times 3\text{cm} = 19.5\text{cm}^2$$

square units for area

There is a different formula for finding the area of each different shape. Substitute given values into the formula.

a triangle: $A = \frac{1}{2} \times b \times h = \frac{1}{2} bh$

h is perpendicular height

b parallelogram: $A = b \times h = bh$

c trapezium: $A = \frac{1}{2} \times (a + b) \times h = \frac{1}{2}(a + b)h$

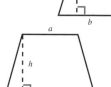

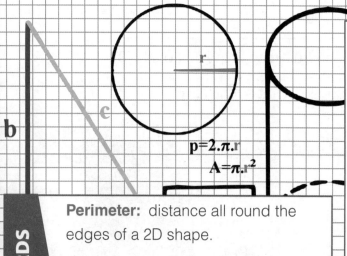

$p = 2.\pi.r$
$A = \pi.r^2$

KEYWORDS

Perimeter: distance all round the edges of a 2D shape.

Area: total surface of a shape.

Volume: amount of space in a 3D shape. The quantity of space a shape holds is called its **capacity**.

Draw a rectangle on squared pap[...]
Count the number of squares in the rectangle.
Measure the length and width of the rectangle.
Multiply them together to find the area.
Is this the same as the number of squares?

Volume

There is a different formula for finding the volume of each different solid. Substitute given values into the formula.

a cube: $V = s \times s \times s = s^3$

b cuboid: $V = l \times w \times h = lwh$

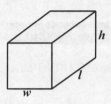

c prism: V = area of cross-section $\times\ l$

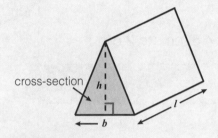

cross-section

EXAMPLE

Volume (V) of a cuboid = $l \times w \times h = lwh$

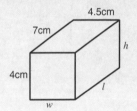

$V = 7 \times 4.5 \times 4 = 126\text{cm}^3$ ← cubed units for volume

Surface area

Calculate the area of each face (side) of a solid shape. Add all these areas together to find the surface area.

EXAMPLE

A cuboid has three pairs of equal faces.

Surface area of the cuboid above:
$2(7 \times 4.5) + 2(4 \times 4.5) + 2(4 \times 7) = 2(31.5 + 18 + 28)$
$$= 2 \times 77.5$$
$$= 155\text{cm}^2$$

1. Work out the perimeter and area of these shapes.
   - **(i)** Square: side 6cm
   - **(ii)** Rectangle: length 5.3mm, width 3.6mm

2. Work out the area of these shapes.
   - **(i)** Triangle: base 11cm, perpendicular height 5.4cm
   - **(ii)** Parallelogram: base 80mm, perpendicular height 4.4cm

3. A rectangular garden measures 9.5m by 6.8m.
   - **(i)** What is the area of the garden?
   - **(ii)** What length of fencing is needed for one long side and two short sides of the garden?
   - **(iii)** It costs £48 to supply and install 2m of fencing. How much will it cost for the fencing?

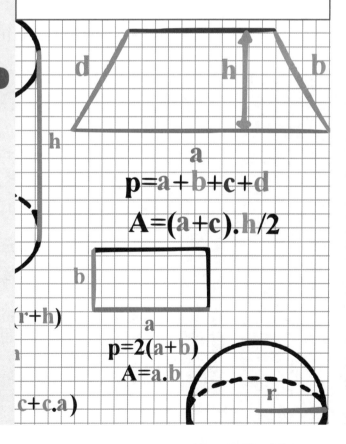

$p = a + b + c + d$

$A = (a + c).h/2$

$p = 2(a + b)$

$A = a.b$

Perimeter and area of a circle

EXAMPLES

a Find the **circumference** and **area of a circle**, **radius** = 4.3cm.

$C = 2\pi r$ $A = \pi r^2$

$= 2\pi(4.3)$ $= \pi(4.3)^2$

$= 27$cm ← to the nearest whole number → $= 58$cm^2

b Find the **diameter** a circle, circumference = 35cm.

$C = \pi d$ → $35 = \pi \times d$ → $d = 35 \div \pi = 11.14$cm (to 2 d.p.)

c Find the radius of a circle, area = 64cm^2.

$A = \pi r^2$ → $64 = \pi \times r^2$ → $r = \sqrt{(64 \div \pi)} = 4.51$cm (to 2 d.p.)

Cylinder

A cylinder is a prism with a circular cross-section.

EXAMPLE

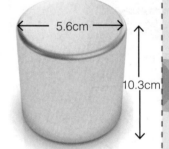

Work out the volume of a cylinder, diameter 5.6cm and length (height) 10.3cm.

diameter = 5.6cm → radius (r) = $\frac{1}{2} \times 5.6$ = 2.8cm

Area of cross-section = $\pi r^2 = \pi(2.8)^2 = 24.63$cm^2 (to 2 d.p.)

Volume of cylinder = area of cross-section × length

$= 24.63... \times 10.3 = 253.689...$

$= 253.7$cm^3 (to 1 d.p.)

KEYWORDS

Radius (r): distance from the centre of a circle to its circumference.

Diameter (d): distance across a circle through its centre. $d = 2r$

Circumference of circle (C): the perimeter of a circle is found using $C = 2\pi r$ or $C = \pi d$

Area of circle (A): $A = \pi r^2$.

Composite shapes = combined shapes

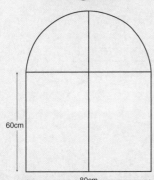

The diagram shows two cupboard doors.

a What area of wood is needed for both doors?

$$A = (60 \times 80) + \frac{1}{2}\pi(40)^2$$
$$= 4800 + 2513.3$$
$$= 7313\text{cm}^2 \text{ to nearest cm}^2$$

b What is the perimeter of the whole opening?

$$P = 80 + 120 + (\frac{1}{2}\pi \times 80)$$
$$= 200 + 126$$
$$= 326\text{cm to nearest cm}$$

25

Draw any circle and mark its centre.
Draw any diameter of this circle. Write down its length d.
Use a length of cotton round the edge of the circle to measure its circumference (C).
Work out $C \div d$.
Repeat for more circles of different sizes.
Comment on the answers to $C \div d$.

1. Find the circumference and area of these circles to the nearest whole number.
   (i) radius = 14mm
   (ii) diameter = 26cm
   (iii) diameter = 6.7cm
   (iv) radius = 1.5m
2. Find the radius of these circles to 2 d.p.
   (i) circumference = 105mm
   (ii) area = 78cm²
   (iii) area = 240mm²
   (iv) circumference = 54cm
3. Work out the capacity of this tin of tomato soup to 3 s.f.

$\leftarrow d = 7\text{cm} \rightarrow$

$h = 11\text{cm}$

4. Work out the area of the shaded part of this photo frame.

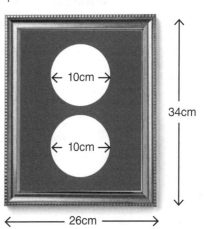

$\leftarrow 10\text{cm} \rightarrow$

$\leftarrow 10\text{cm} \rightarrow$

34cm

$\leftarrow 26\text{cm} \rightarrow$

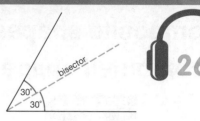

Bisect: divide exactly into two halves.

Perpendicular: at right angles (90°).

Arc: section of circumference of a circle; construction mark made by compasses.

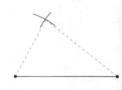

Notation

Label each vertex (point where sides meet) with upper case letters A, B, C.

Label each side opposite an angle with its lower case letter a, b, c.

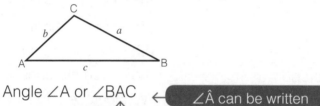

Angle ∠A or ∠BAC

∠Â can be written

angle between sides BA and AC

Constructing triangles

a 3 sides given

Draw side PQ measured to a given length.
Open compasses to length PR and point on P, draw an **arc**.
Open compasses to length QR and point on Q, draw an arc.
Vertex R is where the arcs intersect.

b 2 sides, 1 included angle given

Draw side PQ measured to a given length.
Measure ∠Q using a protractor.
Measure side QR along the line.
Join PR.

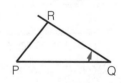

c 1 side, 2 angles given

Draw side PQ measured to a given length.
Measure given angles ∠P and ∠Q using a protractor.
Vertex R is where the angle lines intersect.

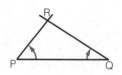

Perpendicular bisector of a line

Draw line EF. With the compasses at a width of over half EF and point on E, draw arcs above and below line EF.
Repeat with the compasses point on F, so that arcs cross at G and H.
GH is the perpendicular bisector of EF → EM = MF (M is the midpoint)
→ ∠EMG = ∠FMG = ∠EMH = ∠FMH = 90°

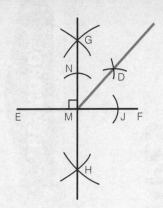

Bisecting angles

Open the compasses to a width to over half MF and, with the point on M, draw arcs to cross MG at N and MF at J.
With the same compass width and point on N and then J, draw arcs to cross at D
→ ∠DMG = ∠DMF = 45°

Perpendicular from point to a line

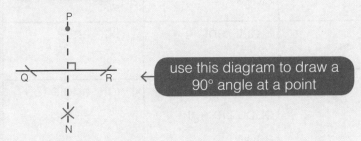

use this diagram to draw a 90° angle at a point

Draw a line. Mark point P above.
With a compass point on P, draw arcs to cross the line at Q and R.
Using the same compass width and point on Q and then R, draw arcs to cross at N below line QR.
Line PN is perpendicular to line QR.
The perpendicular line is the shortest distance from a point to a line.

1. (i) Construct triangle ABC from the given dimensions.
AB = 4.5cm   BC = 5cm
CA = 3cm
   (ii) Measure ∠ACB.
   (iii) If triangle ABC is a diagram drawn to a scale of 1 : 1000, work out the actual measurements of the three sides in metres.

2. (i) Construct triangle PQR from the given dimensions.
PQ = 110mm   PR = 84mm
∠QPR = 40°
   (ii) Measure ∠PRQ and ∠PQR, then add them.

Construct a triangle, XYZ, with each side measuring 5cm.
Measure each angle with a protractor. They should each measure 60°.

With compass width of 3cm and point on X, draw arcs to cross side XY at R and XZ at S.
With the compasses at the same width and point on R and then S, draw arcs to cross at T. Join XT.
Measure ∠TXZ and ∠TXY. These should each be 30° as XT bisects ∠ZXY.

Quadrilateral: a 4-sided shape.

Polygon: a many-sided shape.

Diagonal: a line joining opposite vertices.

Symmetry: a shape has symmetry if it stays the same when reflected or rotated.

Equal sides are shown by short lines across; parallel sides are shown by arrows.

Properties of triangles

Triangle	Example	Sides	Angles
equilateral		3 equal	3 equal
isosceles		2 equal opposite sides	2 equal opposite angles
scalene		3 different	3 different
right angled	Hypotenuse	hypotenuse opposite right angle	1 right angle (90°)

Properties of quadrilaterals

Quadrilateral	Sides	Angles	Diagonals	Lines of symmetry
square	4 equal, 2 pairs parallel	4 equal (90°)	equal and bisect at 90°	4
rectangle	2 opposite pairs parallel and equal	4 equal (90°)	equal and bisect each other	2
parallelogram	2 opposite pairs parallel and equal	2 pairs of opposite angles equal	bisect each other	0
rhombus	4 equal, 2 opposite pairs parallel	2 pairs of opposite angles equal	bisect each other at 90°	2
trapezium	1 pair parallel	4 different	both different	0
isosceles trapezium	1 pair parallel, 1 pair equal	2 pairs of adjacent, equal angles	2 equal	1

Polygons

Polygons are called **regular** if all sides and angles are equal.

Polygon	triangle	quadrilateral	pentagon	hexagon	octagon	decagon
No. of sides	3	4	5	6	8	10

Angles of a 2D shape

a `exterior angle`

An exterior angle of a 2D shape is found by extending a side.

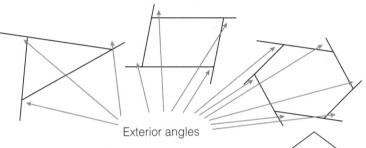

Exterior angles

b `interior angle`

An interior angle of a 2D shape is found between 2 sides.

A circle is also a 2D shape.
← see pages 58–59

Interior angle

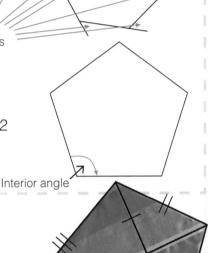

Kite
Sides = 2 pairs of equal, adjacent sides
Diagonals = shorter bisected, intersect at 90°
Angles = 1 pair of opposite angles equal
Lines of symmetry = 1

Draw a polygon with any number of sides greater than 4.
Extend each side in the same direction.
Measure each exterior angle and find their sum.
Measure each interior angle and find their sum.
What is the sum of 1 exterior angle and 1 interior angle?

1. Name the triangles with these properties.
   (i) One 90° angle, 3 different sides
   (ii) 3 different angles, 3 different sides
   (iii) 2 equal angles, 2 equal sides

2. Name the quadrilaterals with these properties.
   (i) 4 equal angles, 2 pairs of equal sides, 2 bisecting diagonals
   (ii) 2 pairs of equal opposite angles, 4 equal sides, 2 bisecting diagonals
   (iii) 2 pairs of equal sides, 2 different diagonals crossing at 90°

3. Name these polygons.
   (i) 8 sides
   (ii) 5 sides
   (iii) 10 sides

4. What should go in the blanks?
   (i) A hexagon has □ sides.
   (ii) A square has □ equal sides and angles and □ diagonals that bisect each other at □.
   (iii) A □ has one pair of parallel sides.

Reflection

EXAMPLE

Describe **reflection** by giving the line of symmetry, e.g. reflect A in $y = 0$

Triangle A is reflected in the x-axis. ← line of symmetry or mirror line is $y = 0$

Triangle B is the reflected image of triangle A (see page 65).

A and B are equidistant from the line of symmetry.

Rotation

EXAMPLE

Describe **rotation** by giving the angle, direction and centre of rotation, e.g. rotate triangle B 90° anticlockwise about (0, 0).

A line is drawn from the centre of rotation to one vertex of triangle B.

An angle of 90° is measured from this line in an anticlockwise direction.

This is repeated for each vertex and triangle C is drawn.

Triangle C is the rotated image of triangle B (see page 65).

The **order of rotational symmetry** is the number of positions a shape can take when rotated through 360° and still look the same.

Translation

Describe **translation** by giving horizontal and vertical distances moved.

This is usually given by a column vector, e.g. $\begin{pmatrix} x \\ y \end{pmatrix}$ where x is horizontal distance and y is vertical distance, e.g. translate C by $\begin{pmatrix} 2 \\ -4 \end{pmatrix}$

Distances **left** and **down** are negative.

Distances **right** and **up** are positive.

Each vertex of triangle C is moved 2 units parallel to the x-axis and −4 units parallel to the y-axis.

Triangle D is the translated image of triangle C (see page 65).

Transformation: moves a shape, sometimes changing its size.

Reflection: produces a mirror image of a shape about a line of symmetry (a mirror line).

Rotation: turns a shape about a point.

Translation: moves a shape in horizontal and vertical directions.

Size and shape stay the same for reflection, rotation and translation.

These are the examples described on page 64:

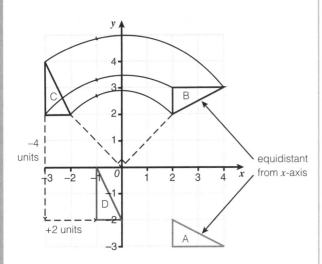

Draw labelled axes on squared paper.
Draw any shape twice on another piece of paper. Cut them out.
Stick one shape in any of the four quadrants.
Use the second shape to reflect, rotate and translate the image.
Write down the descriptions of the **transformations**.

28

Use graph paper for these questions.
Plot points A (2, 1) B (3, 2) C (2, 3) D (1, 2)
Join AB, BC, CD, DA to form a shape.

1. Reflect shape ABCD:

   (i)   in the x-axis   ←label reflected image X

   (ii)   in the y-axis   ←label reflected image Y

   (iii)   in the line $x = 3$ ←label reflected image Z

2. Rotate shape ABCD:

   (i)   through 90° clockwise about (0, 0)   ←label rotated image R

   (ii)   through 180° anticlockwise about (0, 1)   ←label rotated image S

   (iii)   through 90° anticlockwise about (1, 0)   ←label rotated image T

3. Translate shape ABCD by the given column vectors.

   (i) $\begin{pmatrix} 3 \\ 2 \end{pmatrix}$ ←label translated image L

   (ii) $\begin{pmatrix} -2 \\ 2 \end{pmatrix}$ ←label translated image M

   (iii) $\begin{pmatrix} 2 \\ -3 \end{pmatrix}$ ←label translated image N

Congruent triangles

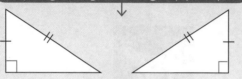

Triangles can be proved congruent if:

3 sides are equal (SSS).

2 sides and their included angle are equal (SAS).

2 angles and their corresponding side are equal (AAS).

Right-angled triangles are congruent if the hypotenuse and 1 side are equal (RHS).

two angles and corresponding side are equal (AAS)

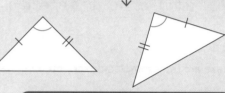

the hypotenuse and one side are equal (in right-angled triangles) (RHS)

two sides and the included angle are equal (SAS)

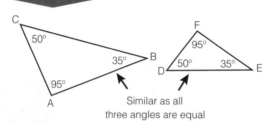

three sides are equal (SSS)

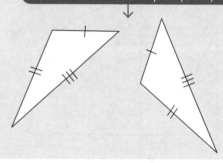

Similar triangles

EXAMPLE

C 50°
35° B
95°
A

F 95°
D 50° 35° E

Similar as all three angles are equal

Triangle ABC is an enlargement of triangle DEF.

Every length in triangle ABC is scale factor × length in triangle DEF.

AB : EF = AC : DF = BC : DE = scale factor (s.f.)

or $\frac{AB}{EF} = \frac{AC}{DF} = \frac{BC}{DE}$ = scale factor

s.f. > 1 ← shape enlarges

s.f. = 1 ← shape stays the same

s.f. < 1 ← shape gets smaller

KEYWORDS

Congruent shapes: shapes that are exactly the same as each other. They have exactly equal angles (corresponding angles) and exactly equal sides (corresponding sides), e.g. a shape and its reflected, rotated or translated images are congruent.

Similar shapes: shapes that have exactly equal angles but are different sizes. Their corresponding sides are in the same ratio.

Enlargement: a transformation by a given scale factor to a similar image.

MODULE 29

Enlargement

Describe **enlargement** by giving the scale factor and the centre of enlargement.

EXAMPLE

Using the origin (0, 0) as centre, enlarge triangle PQR by scale factor 3.

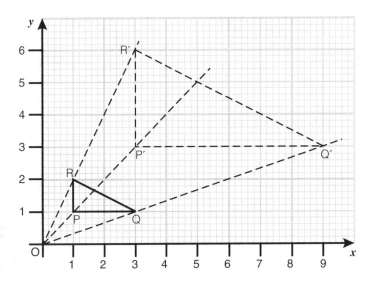

Draw dotted lines from the origin through each vertex.

Mark P′, Q′, R′ so that:

OP′ = 3OP, OQ′ = 3OQ, OR′ = 3OR

Join P′, Q′, R′ to form an enlarged image.

Triangle P′Q′R′ is the enlarged image of triangle PQR.

1. State why these pairs of triangles are congruent.

(i)   (ii)

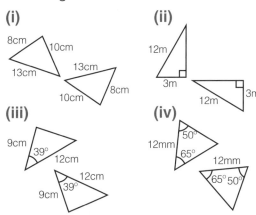

(iii)   (iv)

2. These are pairs of similar triangles. Find the missing sides.

(i)   (ii)

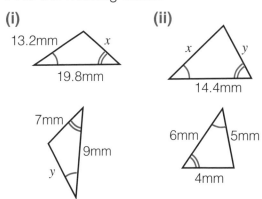

3. On graph paper plot these points.

J (1, 1)   K (2, 1)   L (2, 2)   M (3, 2)
N (3, 3)   P (1, 3)

Join J → K → L → M → N → P → J to form a shape.

Enlarge this shape using the origin (0, 0) as centre and scale factor = 2.

Draw any straight-sided shape on paper.
Enlarge each side by a factor of 2.5.
Draw a dotted line through each pair of corresponding vertices, so they meet at a point.
This point is the centre of enlargement.

TIP

Only the 1st quadrant is needed. Leave plenty of space.

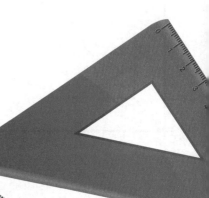

30

Angle: amount of turning measured in degrees, e.g. 55°, 163°, 200°

Types of angles

Angle	Size
acute	$0° < a < 90°$
obtuse	$90° < a < 180°$
reflex	$180° < a < 360°$
right angle	90°

Angle facts

Angles	Name	Fact
	angles at a point	add up to 360° $a + b + c + d = 360°$
	angles on a straight line	add up to 180° $a + b + c = 180°$
	vertically opposite angles	equal: $a = c$, $b = d$

Angles and parallel lines

When a line crosses a set of parallel lines, different types of angles are formed.

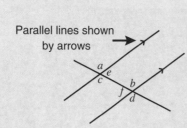

Parallel lines shown by arrows

$a = b$	$c = d$ ← pairs of corresponding angles
$b = c$	$e = f$ ← pairs of alternate angles
$c + f = 180°$	$b + e = 180°$ ← pairs of allied angles
$a = c$	$b = d$ ← pairs of vertically opposite angles

Sum of interior angles of polygons

$a + b + c = 180°$

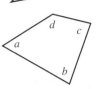

← angle sum of triangle = 180°

$a + b + c + d = 360°$

← angle sum of quadrilateral = 360°

For polygons of five sides or more, divide the polygon into triangles by drawing diagonals from one vertex.

Sum of interior angles of polygon =
180° × number of triangles
number of triangles = number of sides − 2
e.g. sum of interior angles of hexagon = 180° × 4 = 720°

Sum of interior angles of a polygon of n sides = $180°(n - 2)$

Sum of exterior angles of polygons

a Sum of exterior angles of a polygon
= 360°
Each exterior angle of a regular n-sided
polygon = 360° ÷ n

e.g. exterior angle of a regular pentagon
(5 sides) = 360° ÷ 5 = 72°

b $a + d = 180°$ (angles on a straight line)

$a + b + c = 180°$ (angle sum of triangle)
So $d = b + c$
Exterior angle of a triangle = sum of interior opposite
two angles

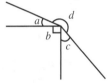

Mark a point P.
Draw five lines from P.
Measure all the angles formed and write them down.
Find the sum of these angles.

1. Use this diagram to answer the following.

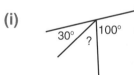

   (i) ☐ is a right angle
   (ii) ☐ make an obtuse angle
   (iii) ☐ are acute angles
   (iv) ☐ is a reflex angle

2. Find the missing angles.

   (i)

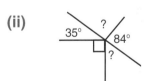

   (ii)

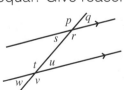

3. Which pairs of angles are equal? Give reasons.

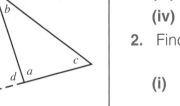

KEYWORDS

Pythagoras' theorem: Use in a right-angled triangle if only sides are involved:

square on the hypotenuse = sum of the squares on the other two sides

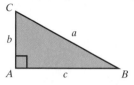

$$a^2 = b^2 + c^2$$

a is hypotenuse – always longest side

Trigonometry ratios: Use in a right-angled triangle if angles and sides are involved:

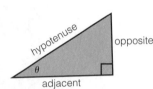

$$\sin \theta = \frac{\text{opposite}}{\text{hypotenuse}}$$
$$\cos \theta = \frac{\text{adjacent}}{\text{hypotenuse}}$$
$$\tan \theta = \frac{\text{opposite}}{\text{adjacent}}$$

The sine, cosine and tangent ratios show the relationships between the sides of a triangle.

Using Pythagoras' theorem to find a side

EXAMPLES

a Work out the length of BC.

$BC^2 = AB^2 + AC^2$ ← Pythagoras' theorem

$= 8^2 + 15^2$ ← substitute in given sides

$= 64 + 225 = 289$

So BC = $\sqrt{289}$ = 17cm

b Work out the length of MN.

$LN^2 = MN^2 + LM^2$ ← Pythagoras' theorem

$8^2 = MN^2 + 4^2$ ← substitute in given sides

$64 = MN^2 + 16$ → $MN^2 = 64 - 16 = 48$

So MN = $\sqrt{48}$ = 6.9cm (2 s.f.)

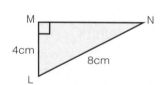

Special right-angled triangles have sides in ratio: 3 : 4 : 5; 5 : 12 : 13; 8 : 15 : 17; 7 : 24 : 25

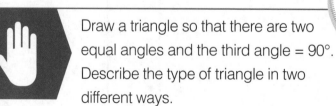

Draw a triangle so that there are two equal angles and the third angle = 90°.
Describe the type of triangle in two different ways.
Measure the two shorter sides.
Use Pythagoras' theorem to find the third side.

Using Pythagoras' theorem to prove a triangle is right-angled

EXAMPLES

Substitute the lengths of the sides in Pythagoras' theorem. If it works, the triangle is right-angled.

a

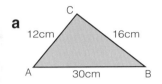

$$AB^2 = 30^2 = 900$$
$$AC^2 + BC^2 = 12^2 + 16^2 = 144 + 256 = 400$$
So ABC is not a right-angled triangle.
$$AB^2 \neq AC^2 + BC^2$$

b

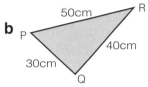

$$PR^2 = 50^2 = 2500$$
$$PQ^2 + QR^2 = 30^2 + 40^2 = 900 + 1600 = 2500$$
So PQR is a right-angled triangle.
$$PR^2 = PQ^2 + QR^2$$

Using trigonometry ratios to find the length of a side

EXAMPLE

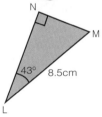

$$\sin 43° = \frac{MN}{LM} = \frac{MN}{8.5} \leftarrow \begin{array}{l}\text{opposite} \\ \text{hypotenuse}\end{array}$$

So MN = 8.5 × sin 43° = 5.796 = 5.8cm (to 1 d.p.)

↑ using calculator 'sin' key

Using trigonometry ratios to find an angle

EXAMPLE

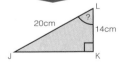

$$\cos L = \frac{KL}{JL} = \frac{14}{20} \leftarrow \begin{array}{l}\text{adjacent} \\ \text{hypotenuse}\end{array}$$

$$\cos L = 0.7 \rightarrow \angle L = \cos^{-1} 0.7 \leftarrow \begin{array}{l}\text{inverse cos – use} \\ \text{shift for } \cos^{-1} \text{ key}\end{array}$$

So ∠L = 45.6° ← angles given to 1 d.p.

1. Find the missing side in each of these triangles. Give your answers correct to 1 d.p. where necessary.

   (i)

   (ii)

   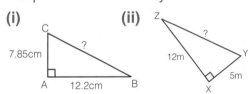

2. Are these triangles right-angled?
   (i) AB = 33mm, BC = 44mm, AC = 55mm
   (ii) AB = 1.9m, BC = 2.3m, AC = 3.4m

3. Find the missing side or angle in each of the following. Give your answers correct to 1 d.p.

   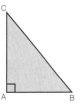

   (i) BC = 47, ∠B = 62° , AB = ?
   (ii) BC = 32, ∠B = 73°, AC = ?
   (iii) AB = 63.4, BC = 150, ∠C = ?

Properties of cubes and cuboids

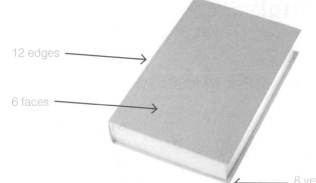

12 edges

6 faces

8 vertices

A cube is a cuboid with all edges equal.

Properties of prisms

Prisms take their name from their **cross-section**.

Prism		Faces	Edges	Vertices
triangular		5	9	6
hexagonal		8	18	12
circular = cylinder		3	2	0

Properties of pyramids

A tetrahedron has 4 equal triangular faces.

Pyramids take their name from the shape of their base.

Pyramid		Faces	Edges	Vertices
square-based		5	8	5
triangular-based		4	6	4
circular = cone		2	1	1

3D shape (or solid): has three dimensions: length, width, height.

Face: a side of a 3D shape.

Edge: where two faces meet.

Vertex (pl. vertices): corners where edges meet.

Cross-section: shape shown when a solid is cut at right angles.

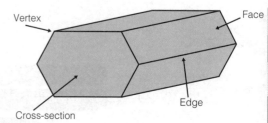

Vertex

Face

Edge

Cross-section

Properties of a sphere

Solid		Faces	Edges	Vertices
sphere		1	0	0
hemisphere		2	1	0

Formulae for solving problems with 3D shapes

a surface area (SA)

b volume (V)

Cone: SA (curved surface) = $\pi r l$

$V = \frac{1}{3}\pi r^2 h$

slant height

Cylinder: SA = $2\pi r h + 2\pi r^2$

$V = \pi r^2 h$

ends

Pyramid: SA depends on no. of faces to be added.

$V = \frac{1}{3} \times$ base area $\times h$

Sphere: SA = $4\pi r^2$

$V = \frac{4}{3}\pi r^3$

1. Name a solid shape which has:
   (i) 5 faces, 8 edges, 5 vertices
   (ii) 2 faces, 1 edge, 1 vertex
   (iii) 6 equal faces, 12 equal edges, 8 vertices
   (iv) 5 faces, 9 edges, 6 vertices

2. An ice-cream cone has diameter = 4cm and perpendicular height = 9cm.
   The ice-cream is level with the top of the cone.
   How much ice-cream does the cone hold?

3. A solid shape is made up of a cylinder and a hemisphere fitting exactly on the end.
   The cylinder has radius 3cm, height 7cm.
   Work out the surface area and volume of the whole shape.

Draw a 2cm square on squared paper. Label it 1. Draw one 2cm square above and touching square 1, and another 2cm square below and touching square 1. Label these squares 2 and 3.

Draw a 2cm square on each side, touching square 1. Label them 4 and 5.

Now draw another 2cm square at the side of and touching square 5.

The combined shape should look like a 'T' on its side.

Cut out the 'T' shape and fold along the touching sides to form a cube.

The shape you have drawn is called a **net** of the cube.

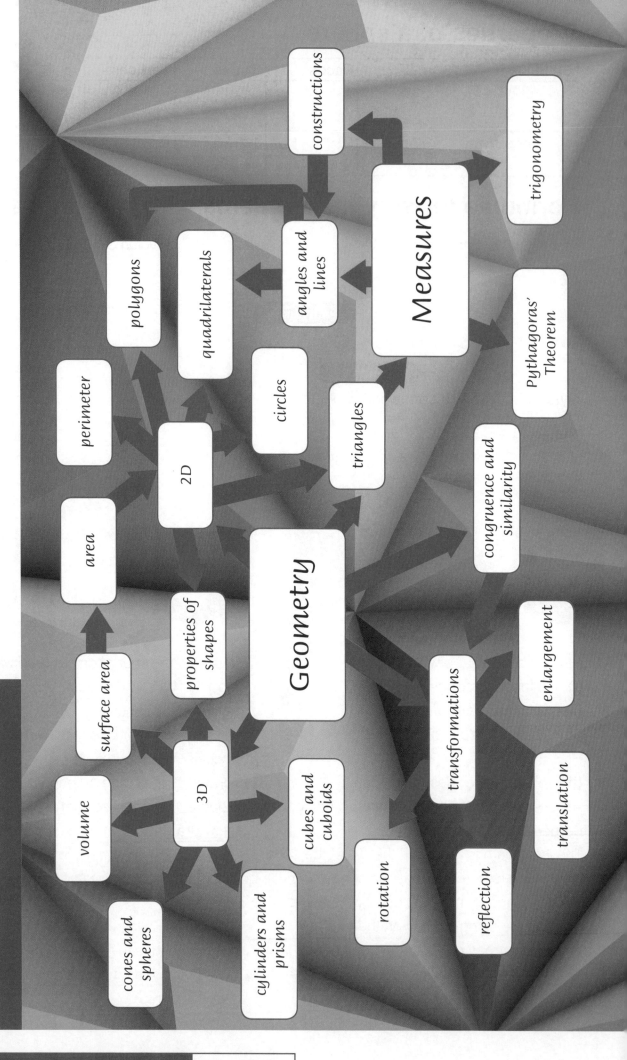

constructions

trigonometry

Measures

angles and lines

polygons

quadrilaterals

circles

triangles

Pythagoras' Theorem

perimeter

2D

congruence and similarity

area

enlargement

properties of shapes

Geometry

surface area

transformations

translation

volume

3D

cubes and cuboids

rotation

reflection

cones and spheres

cylinders and prisms

1. Two triangles are fitted together to make other shapes.

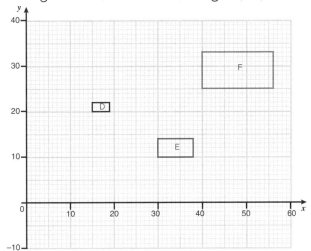

a Work out whether either triangle is right-angled. **[2]**

b Make three different shapes using both triangles combined.

Write down the perimeter of each combined shape. **[3]**

c Find the area of triangle DEF. **[1]**

d Work out ∠A and ∠C. **[2]**

2. A china mug is a cylinder with a diameter of 7cm. It is filled with tea up to a height of 9.8cm.

a How much tea does the mug hold to the nearest whole number? **[1]**

b A teapot holds 1.5 litres of tea. Approximately how many mugs of tea can be poured from the teapot? **[1]**

c Another teapot has a capacity which is $\frac{2}{3}$ of the first teapot. A tea cup holds 175ml of tea.

Approximately how many cups of tea can be poured from the second teapot? **[1]**

3. This diagram shows three rectangles, D, E and F.

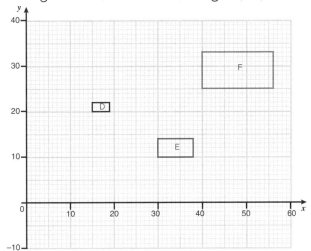

Copy and complete this table. **[2]**

Enlargement	Centre of enlargement	Scale factor
D → E	(3, 29)	2
E → F		
F → D		

EXPERIMENTAL PROBABILITY

MODULE 33

Probability

Probability (P) = number of times event can happen ÷ total number of possible **outcomes**

↑ probability is usually given as a fraction, but can be decimal or %

> A fair dice has $\frac{1}{6}$ chance of landing on each number 1–6. A biased dice will not produce this outcome.

EXAMPLES

A fair dice is thrown.

a $P(5) = \frac{1}{6}$ ← number of times 5 can occur
← number of possible outcomes

b $P(\text{odd number}) = \frac{3}{6}$ ← number of odd numbers
← number of possible outcomes

$= \frac{1}{2}$ ← simplify to lowest terms

Probability scale

> It is useful to know what's in a pack of playing cards.

EXAMPLES

a certain outcome: $P = 1$ $P(\text{April following March}) = 1$

b likely outcome: $0.5 < P < 1$ $P(\text{at least 3 rainy days in November})$
$= \frac{4}{5}$ or 0.8 or 80%

c evens: $P = 0.5$ $P(\text{tail when tossing a coin})$
$= \frac{1}{2}$ or 0.5 or 50%

d unlikely: $0 < P < 0.5$ $P(\text{picking an Ace from a pack of cards})$
$= \frac{4}{52} = \frac{1}{13}$ or 0.08 or 8%

e impossible: $P = 0$ $P(\text{scoring 2.5 when throwing two dice})$
$= 0$ ← must be a whole number

KEYWORDS

Probability: the chance an event may happen.

Outcome: the result of an event happening.

Probability scale: probability ranges from impossible (0) to certain (1).

Unlikely		Likely
0	**0.5**	**1**
Impossible	Evens	Certain

Total probability

Sum of the probabilities of all possible outcomes = 1

EXAMPLE

A dice is thrown.

$P(\text{even number}) = \frac{3}{6} = \frac{1}{2}$ $P(\text{odd number}) = \frac{3}{6} = \frac{1}{2}$

So sum of all possible outcomes = $\frac{1}{2} + \frac{1}{2} = 1$ as it is certain that a number (even or odd) will be thrown.

Probability of an event not happening

$P(\text{event will happen}) + P(\text{event will not happen}) = 1$

So $P(\text{event will not happen}) = 1 - P(\text{event will happen})$

Toss a coin 10 times. Record H(head) or T(tail) in a table.

Toss the coin another 10 times. Record H or T in the table.

Carry on tossing the coin until it has been tossed 50 times, recording H or T each time. Count the number of H and the number of T.

Divide each by 50. Comment on the results. Predict the results after tossing the coin 100 times.

1. All red cards are removed from a pack of 52 cards. Write down if it is certain, impossible, evens, likely or unlikely that a card picked at random from the pack will be:
   (i) the Ace of Spades (ii) a Club
   (iii) a red card (iv) a black card

2. All the letters of the alphabet are written on separate cards. One card is picked at random. Work out the following probabilities:
   (i) $P(\text{consonant})$ (ii) $P(\text{vowel})$
   (iii) $P(\text{a letter of the alphabet})$
   (iv) $P(\text{any number})$

3. A dice is thrown. Work out the following probabilities:
   (i) $P(\text{even number})$ (ii) $P(\text{odd number})$
   (iii) $P(\text{multiple of 3})$ (iv) $P(\text{prime})$

4. Draw a probability scale. Mark the following probabilities with arrows:
   (i) Having a birthday before this time next year.
   (ii) Tossing a coin and getting a Tail.
   (iii) Winning a lottery prize.
   (iv) Snow in December.

Single events

EXAMPLES

A bag holds 3 yellow balls, 4 blue balls, 5 red balls and 8 black balls. If a ball is picked at **random** and then replaced, find the probability of picking the following.

a yellow ball: P(yellow) = $\frac{3}{20}$ ← number of yellow balls
← total number of balls

b black ball: P(black) = $\frac{8}{20}$ = $\frac{2}{5}$ ← give in lowest terms

c white ball: P(white) = 0   ← impossible as there are no white balls

d red ball or blue ball: P(red or blue)

= $\frac{5}{20}$ + $\frac{4}{20}$ = $\frac{9}{20}$ ← **mutually exclusive events** so add the probabilities

Combined events

EXAMPLES

a dependent   ← event dependent on previous event

e.g. A red ball is picked from the bag in the example above. It is not replaced. A blue ball is then picked.

P(red ball) = $\frac{5}{20}$ = $\frac{1}{4}$ ← number of blue balls

P(blue ball) = $\frac{4}{19}$ ← total number of remaining balls

b independent   ← outcome of an event does not affect the outcome of any further event

Multiply separate probabilities to find combined probability.

e.g. A coin is tossed and a dice is thrown. What is the probability of throwing a Head and a 3?

TIP
P(A) or P(B) = P(A) + P(B)
P(A) and P(B) = P(A) × P(B)

P(Head) = $\frac{1}{2}$ P(3) = $\frac{1}{6}$

So P(H and 3) = $\frac{1}{2}$ × $\frac{1}{6}$ = $\frac{1}{12}$

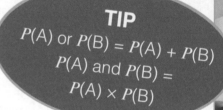

Sample space

Letters A, B, C and numbers 1, 2, 3, 4 are written on pieces of card.

All possible outcomes of picking a letter and a number are shown.

	1	2	3	4
A	A1	A2	A3	A4
B	B1	B2	B3	B4
C	C1	C2	C3	C4

Total number of outcomes = $3 \times 4 = 12$

$P(3, B) = \frac{1}{12}$; $P(\text{even, C}) = \frac{2}{12} = \frac{1}{6}$

Tree diagram

A fair coin is thrown twice.

All possible outcomes are shown on branches.

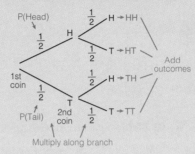

$P(\text{Head})$

$\frac{1}{2}$ H → HH

$\frac{1}{2}$ H

$\frac{1}{2}$ T → HT

Add outcomes

1st coin

$\frac{1}{2}$ H → TH

$\frac{1}{2}$ T

$P(\text{Tail})$ 2nd coin $\frac{1}{2}$ T → TT

Multiply along branch

$P(\text{HH}) = \frac{1}{2} \times \frac{1}{2} = \frac{1}{4}$

$P(\text{TT}) = \frac{1}{2} \times \frac{1}{2} = \frac{1}{4}$

$\left. \right\}$ $P(\text{both same}) = \frac{1}{4} + \frac{1}{4} = \frac{1}{2}$

Draw a sample space table to display all the possible outcomes of throwing two dice. Write down the following using the sample space table.

a total number of outcomes

b $P(2 \text{ even numbers})$

c $P(\text{combined total being a prime})$

1. A bag contains 9 black balls and 6 white balls. A ball is picked out of the bag at random and not replaced. This is repeated. Using a probability tree, work out the following probabilities:
   (i) $P(\text{ball of each colour})$
   (ii) $P(2 \text{ balls the same colour})$
   (iii) $P(\text{not a black ball})$

2. Two coins are tossed. Draw a sample space table to display all possible outcomes. Find the following probabilities:
   (i) $P(2 \text{ Heads})$ (ii) $P(\text{not getting a Head})$

3. Each letter of the word PROBABILITY is written on a piece of card. Work out the following probabilities:
   (i) $P(\text{B or I})$ (ii) $P(\text{vowel or a consonant})$
   (iii) $P(\text{letter in first half of alphabet})$
   (iv) $P(\text{letter in the word ALSO})$

4. A fair dice is thrown twice. Work out the following probabilities:
   (i) $P(2 \text{ or } 5)$
   (ii) $P(\text{not throwing a 3 either time})$
   (iii) $P(3 \text{ and } 4)$ (iv) $P(\text{even both times})$

KEYWORDS

Random event: event happening by chance or without bias.

Mutually exclusive events: events that cannot happen at the same time.

Sample space diagram: diagram displaying all possible outcomes of two events.

Tree diagram: diagram displaying all possible outcomes of two or more events.

Union of sets (∪)

🎧 35

Set A ∪ B contains all members belonging to A or B or both.

EXAMPLE

If A = {2, 3, 4} and B = {4, 5, 6, 7},
then A ∪ B = {2, 3, 4, 5, 6, 7}

← all members in both sets

A and B are **finite sets** – they have a restricted number of members. The set of integers {... –2, –1, 0, 1, 2, 3...} is an example of an **infinite set** – it has no end.

Intersection of sets (∩)

Set A ∩ B contains members belonging to both A and B.

EXAMPLE

If A = {2, 3, 4} and B = {1, 3, 5}, then A ∩ B = {3}.

← only member in both sets

If A and B have no members in common, then A ∩ B = ∅.

← empty set

Venn diagrams

Relationships between sets can be shown on a Venn diagram.

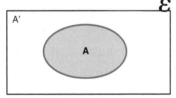 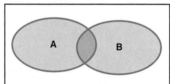 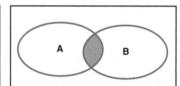

a A + A′ = $\mathcal{E}$ e.g. A = {1, 3, 5, 7, 9}

A′ = {2, 4, 6, 8, 10}

$\mathcal{E}$ = {1, 2, 3, ..., 10}

b A ∪ B   e.g. A = {3, 6, 9, 12, 15}

B = {2, 4, 6, 8, 10}

A ∪ B = {2, 3, 4, 6, 8, 9, 10, 12, 15}

c A ∩ B   e.g. A = {3, 6, 9, 12, 15, 18}   ← multiples of 3

B = {2, 4, 6, 8, 10, 12}   ← multiples of 2

A ∩ B = {6, 12}   ← multiples of 6

1. A and B are **subsets** of the **universal set** $\mathcal{E}$.

   $\mathcal{E}$ = {months of the year}

   A = {months beginning with J}

   B = {months with 31 days}

   (i) List the members of A ∩ B.

   (ii) List the members of A ∪ B.

   (iii) Draw a Venn diagram to illustrate $\mathcal{E}$, A and B.

2. A and B are subsets of the universal set $\mathcal{E}$.

   $\mathcal{E}$ = {numbers from 1 to 30}

   A = {factors of 15}

   B = {factors of 30}

   (i) List the members of A ∩ B.

   (ii) List the members of A ∪ B.

   (iii) Draw a Venn diagram to illustrate $\mathcal{E}$, A and B.

3. The Venn diagram shows universal set $\mathcal{E}$ = {number of pupils in class 9B} and subsets:

   A = {number of pupils in school football team}

   B = {number of pupils in school swimming team}

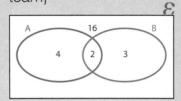

   (i) How many pupils are in each team?

   (ii) How many pupils are in both teams?

   (iii) How many pupils are not in the football team?

   (iv) How many pupils are in neither team?

Take a pack of cards. Divide the pack into

Set A → {all red cards}

Set B → {all black cards}

Set A ∩ B → {all picture cards}

Draw a Venn diagram to illustrate the above.

How many cards are in set A ∪ B?

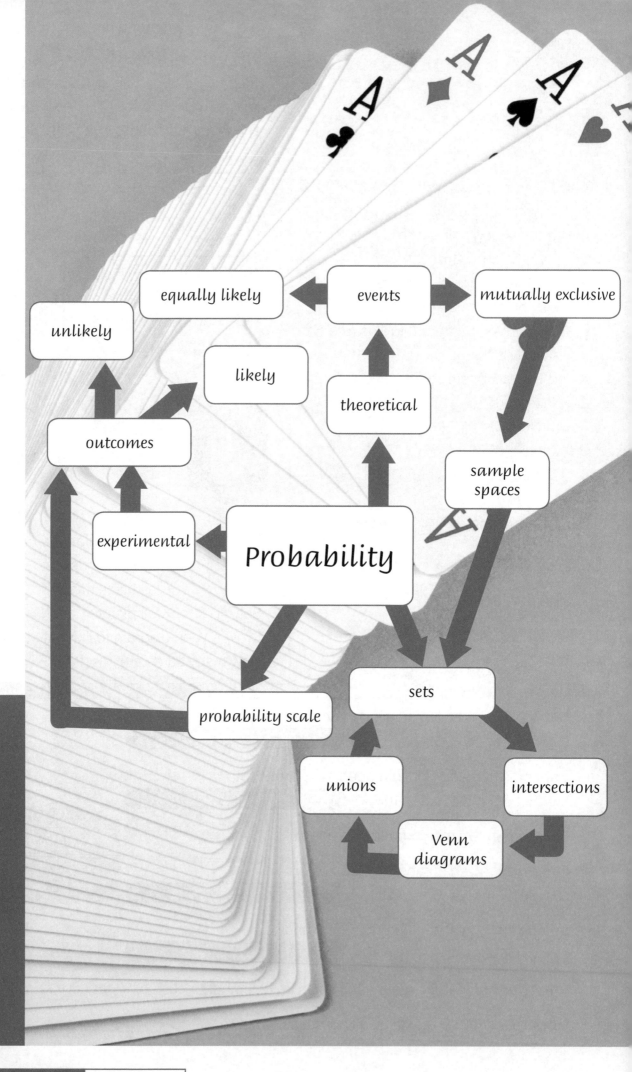

equally likely

unlikely

likely

events

mutually exclusive

outcomes

theoretical

experimental

Probability

sample spaces

probability scale

sets

unions

intersections

Venn diagrams

1. A game of Snakes and Ladders has 100 squares.

   If a counter lands on the head of a snake, the player has to return to the tail-end of the snake.

   If a counter lands on the bottom of a ladder, the player can climb to the top of the ladder.

   There are 8 snake heads and 8 ladders.

   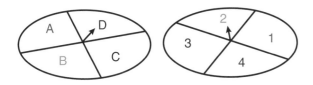

   a What is the probability of landing on a snake head? [1]

   b What is the probability of not landing at the bottom of a ladder? [1]

   c What is the probability of not landing on either? [1]

2. Here are two spinners.

   a Draw a sample space to display all possible outcomes. [4]

   b What is the probability of spinning a vowel with an odd number? [1]

   c What is the probability of spinning a consonant with a multiple of 2? [1]

3. This Venn diagram shows the number of Year 9 students studying French, German and Spanish.

   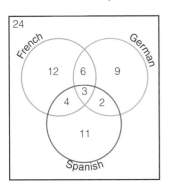

   a How many students study:

   i   French and German? [1]   iii all three languages? [1]

   ii Spanish and German? [1]   iv none of the three languages? [1]

   b How many students are in Year 9? [1]

Collecting data

a Observation

36

EXAMPLE

Investigate vehicles passing a school between 11am and 12 noon.

Method:
→ list possible vehicles
→ divide time into short periods
→ check vehicles going both ways

Record: ← data collection sheet like a tally chart

e.g. Mark as shown: I for each vehicle;
use ⪢⪢⪢ to represent 5 ← easier to count

Vehicle	Bike	Motorbike	Car	Bus	Taxi	Van	Lorry	Other
11.00–11.15	I I I							
11.16–11.30	I I							
11.31–11.45	I I I							
11.46–12.00	⪢⪢⪢ I							

↑ make sure group limits do not overlap

b Questionnaire ← set of questions used to find data

EXAMPLE

Conduct a survey to find which TV programmes people prefer.

Questions should be easy to understand and unbiased.

Questions should be asked in a logical order.

Response boxes are useful, e.g. yes ☐ no ☐

Survey is only valid if a large enough sample is questioned.
Sample size $\geq$ 20 is usually recommended.

c Frequency table ← organises **raw data** in columns

EXAMPLE

frequency found by adding tally marks ↓

Vehicle	Frequency (*f*)
bike	14
motorbike	6
car	32
bus	5
↓	↓

Conduct a survey to find out people's favourite snacks.

Follow this plan:

Write a questionnaire of a minimum of six questions.

Use a minimum sample of 20.

Organise your results into a frequency table.

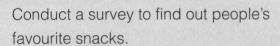

Colour of eyes	Blue	Brown	Green	Other
Girls	JHT JHT II	JHT JHT III	III	II
Boys	JHT IIII	JHT JHT JHT	II	I

1. Are the following **discrete**, **continuous** or **grouped** data?

   (i) Types of drinks sold at a café during one week.

   (ii) Times of marathon runners at the last Olympic Games.

   (iii) Shoe sizes sold by a shoe shop in one month.

   (iv) Age categories of members of a gym.

2. This is a tally chart of collected data from two classes in a school.

Colour of eyes	Blue	Brown	Green	Other
Girls	JHT JHT II	JHT JHT III	III	II
Boys	JHT IIII	JHT JHT JHT	II	I

   (i) Transfer the information into a frequency table.

   (ii) Write down the total number of girls in the two classes.

   (iii) Write down the total number of pupils questioned.

3. The school library decides to survey its borrowers about how they use the library. The first draft of the questionnaire used the following questions. Explain why these questions are unsuitable and rewrite them.

   (i) How old are you?

   (ii) When do you use the library?

   (iii) What books do you like to read?

   (iv) How many books do you borrow?

KEYWORDS	**Average:** a typical or representative value.
	Mean: average value using the sum of all the values.
	Median: average value using middle term of ascending values.
	Mode: most frequent value.
	Range: a measure of the spread of the data.

Mean

Mean = total sum of values ÷ number of values

EXAMPLES

a Work out the mean of the values in this list:

16.3mm, 14.6mm, 18.4mm, 21.3mm, 19mm

Mean = (16.3 + 14.6 + 18.4 + 21.3 + 19) ÷ 5 = 17.9mm

Always check:

→ all values are in the same units

→ the mean average lies between the smallest and the largest values.

b Find the mean of the following set of data:

Weight (kg)	62	63	64	65	66
Frequency	3	5	6	6	5

$$\text{Mean} = \frac{(62 \times 3) + (63 \times 5) + (64 \times 6) + (65 \times 6) + (66 \times 5)}{25}$$

$$= 1605 \div 25 = 64.2\text{kg}$$

> → If data is in a frequency table, use value × frequency to get all values.

Median

EXAMPLES

a Odd number of values: 33kg, 32kg, 35kg, 35kg, 38kg, 30kg, 34kg

Arrange values in ascending order: 30kg, 32kg, 33kg, 34kg, 35kg, 35kg, 38kg

↑ middle value

So median = 34kg

b Even number of values: 24mins, 23mins, 24mins, 21mins, 22mins, 24mins

Arrange values in ascending order: 21mins, 22mins, 23mins, 24mins, 24mins, 24mins

↑ middle value is halfway between 23 and 24

So median = 23.5mins

Mode

Find the mode of these values:

1, 3, 0, 2, 2, 2, 3, 0, 4, 0, 5, 2

So mode = 2 as it is the most frequent value.

Range

Range = greatest value − least value

Find the range of these values:

2.4m, 1.6m, 4.3m, 0.25m, 3.5m, 4.8m

greatest value   least value

So range = 4.8m − 0.25m = 4.55m

Using the appropriate average

Mean → used most often as uses all values.

Median → useful for ignoring extreme values.

Mode → gives most frequently occurring value.

Spread your hand to make a span.
Measure your handspan.
Measure the handspans of five other people.
Find the mean, median and range of the handspans.

Find the mean, median, mode and range of each of the following sets of data in questions 1, 2 and 3.

1. (i) 22, 30, 32, 41, 30, 31
   (ii) 87, 90, 95, 74, 69, 77, 89, 92, 76, 90
   (iii) 8, 10, 6, 8, 4, 3, 11, 7, 5
2. (i) £42, £50, £42, £42, £50, £38
   (ii) 83p, 90p, 86p, 83p, 84p, 83p, 90p, 87p, 86p
   (iii) €167, €172, €164, €173, €172, €152
3. (i) 52cm, 53cm, 53cm, 51cm, 53cm, 51cm
   (ii) 287g, 290g, 290g, 274g, 269g, 277g, 189g, 192g, 277g, 290g
   (iii) 81ml, 81ml, 86ml, 78ml, 84ml, 81ml, 80ml, 78ml, 86ml
4. Find the mean of the following set of data.

Height (cm)	162	163	164	165	166
Frequency	3	5	8	8	6

Pictogram: uses pictures to represent the number of items.

Bar chart: uses vertical or horizontal bars (equal width) to represent items; frequency given by the length of a bar. A line can be used instead of a bar.

Pie chart: uses angles in a circular chart to represent values in proportion.

Scatter graph: compares two sets of data.
Relationship is called **correlation**.

38

Stem and leaf diagram: uses stem with leaves to display data and show distribution.

Pictogram

EXAMPLE

Data about pets visiting a vet in one day

Key should be given,

e.g. Each animal represents 3 pets:

$\frac{1}{3}$ of pet represents 1; $\frac{2}{3}$ of pet represents 2.

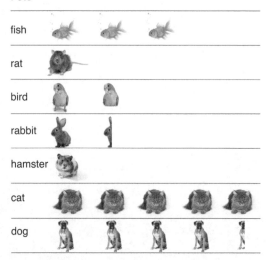

Bar chart

EXAMPLE

Data about library users

Compare more than one set of data by drawing bars for each set next to one another.
Label to show what the bars represent.

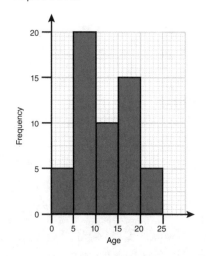

Pie chart

EXAMPLE

Each item is represented by the angle found by (frequency ÷ total no. items) × 360°.
Draw a circle and mark its centre.
Draw a radius and measure the angle for each colour.
Write the name on each slice of the pie chart.

Data about favourite colour

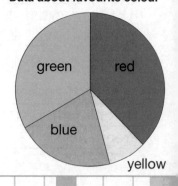

Scatter graph

Data about test marks for Maths and Physics.

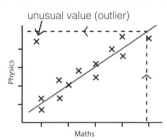

Each pair of marks gives the coordinates of a point, marked with a cross.

Draw a 'line of best fit' through the approximate middle of the points:

→ data increases together

+ve correlation (upwards slope)

→ one set of data increases as the other decreases

−ve correlation (downwards slope)

Use the line of best fit to estimate data not given. It cannot be drawn if all points are scattered.

Stem and leaf diagram

Data about English test marks.

Key: 1 | 5 = 15

0	8
1	5 6 7
2	0 0 2 2 5 7 9
3	0

Stem formed by 'tens' digit.
Leaf formed by 'units' digit.
Marks put in order before doing diagram.

soon...

Look at the TV schedule for a day.
Make a frequency table for different types of programmes.
Draw a bar chart to illustrate the different types of programmes.
Repeat for another day, drawing the second day's bars alongside the bars for the first day.
Compare the programmes for the two days.

1. A survey of car colours produced this frequency table.
   Draw a pictogram to illustrate this data, choosing a picture to represent four cars.

Car colour	black	white	silver	blue	red
Frequency	8	22	20	14	6

2. Some pet-owners were asked about their favourite pets. The survey produced this frequency table.
   Calculate the angles and draw a pie chart to illustrate this data.

Favourite pet	cat	dog	fish	rabbit
Frequency	15	18	5	2

3. The length and width of some leaves were measured.
   Plot the data on a scatter graph. Use a line of best fit to find the missing measurements **a** and **b**.

Length (mm)	47	28	70	36	60	35	20	56	30	b
Width (mm)	20	17	42	21	35	20	27	33	a	45

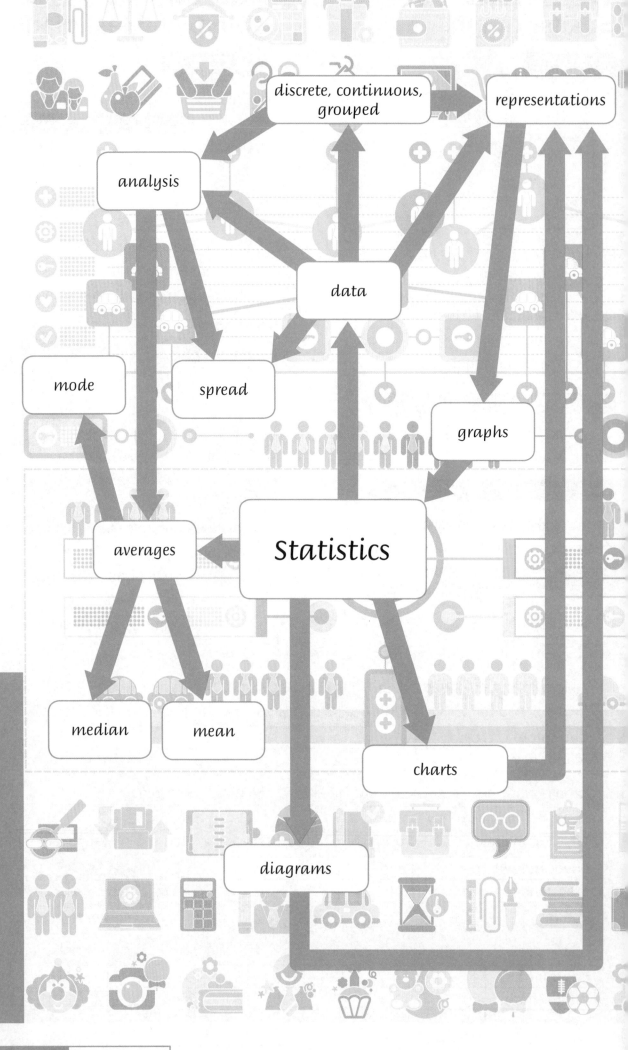

discrete, continuous, grouped

representations

analysis

data

mode

spread

graphs

averages

Statistics

median

mean

charts

diagrams

1. A multiplex cinema wants to find out about its audiences over a three-month period.

   a What data is needed? **[2]**

   b Which people could be questioned? **[1]**

   c Suggest five questions for the survey. **[5]**

2. This table gives the number of goals scored, each month during a season, by a football team.

Month	Aug	Sept	Oct	Nov	Dec	Jan	Feb	Mar	Apr	May
Goals	3	5	8	7	4	4	6	4	5	6

   a What is the team's modal number of goals per month? **[1]**

   b What is the team's mean monthly score during the season? **[1]**

   c If the team plays four games every month, what is the mean number of goals scored each game? **[1]**

3. This is a stem and leaf diagram showing results (%) in an end-of-term Maths test.

```
2 | 4  9
3 | 6  8  9              Key: 3 | 6 = 36%
4 | 3  4  8
5 | 1  3  3  3  9  9
6 | 0  2  4  7  9
7 | 1  3  5
8 | 0  3
9 | 2
```

   a How many students are in this Maths group? **[1]**

   b What is the modal Maths mark? **[1]**

   c What is the range of marks in the group? **[1]**

   d Work out the mean and median marks. **[2]**

   e Which is the most appropriate average for the teacher to use? **[1]**

NUMBER

Module 1

Quick test questions

1. (i) > (ii) < (iii) ≠ (iv) = (v) ≤ (vi) ≥

2.

```
   -5  -4  -3  -2  -1   0   1   2   3   4   5
           ↑   ↑   ↑               ↑   ↑   ↑
```

3. (i) < (ii) > (iii) > (iv) < (v) > (vi) =

4. (i) 3 (ii) $\frac{3}{1000}$ (iii) 400 (iv) $\frac{6}{10}$

Module 2

Quick test questions

1. (i) 15: 1, 3, 5, 15; 18: 1, 2, 3, 6, 9, 18 (ii) HCF = 3

2. (i) 9,18, 27, 36, 45; 36, 72, 108, 144, 180
(ii) LCM = 36

3. (i) 11, 13, 17, 19, 23 (ii) 31, 37, 41, 43

4. (i) $2 \times 2 \times 3 \times 5$ (ii) $3 \times 3 \times 7$

Module 3

Quick test questions

1. (i) 994 (ii) 25 (iii) 15.49 (iv) 4938.1
(v) 10 542 (vi) 16.3

2. (i) −36 (ii) −5 (iii) +9 (iv) −30

3. (i) $1\frac{32}{45}$ (ii) $\frac{21}{8}$

4. (i) $\frac{26}{24}$ or $1\frac{2}{24}$ or $1\frac{1}{12}$ (ii) $3\frac{11}{12}$ (iii) $\frac{11}{42}$
(iv) $2\frac{2}{15}$ (v) $\frac{91}{20}$ or $4\frac{11}{20}$ (vi) $\frac{8}{21}$

Module 4

Quick test questions

1. (i) $5 \times 5 \times 5 \times 5 = 625$ (ii) $4 \times 4 \times 4 \times 4 \times 4 = 1024$
(iii) $3 \times 3 \times 3 \times 3 \times 3 \times 3 = 729$
(iv) $2 \times 2 \times 2 \times 2 \times 2 \times 2 \times 2 = 128$
(v) $\frac{1}{2} \times \frac{1}{2} \times \frac{1}{2} = \frac{1}{8}$
(vi) $\frac{1}{1} \times \frac{1}{1} \times \frac{1}{1} \times \frac{1}{1} = 1$

2. (i) 6 (ii) 9 (iii) 7 (iv) 2 (v) 8 (vi) 1

3. (i) y^5 (ii) a^5 (iii) $6c^7$ (iv) $2x$

4. (i) 3.21×10^5 (ii) 4.56×10^{-4} (iii) 6 325 000
(iv) 0.000 000 123

Module 5

Quick test questions

1. (i) 54% (ii) 115% (iii) 60% (iv) 35%

2. (i) $\frac{13}{100}$ (ii) $2\frac{3}{4}$ (iii) $\frac{3}{20}$ (iv) $\frac{4}{25}$

3. (i) 0.32 (ii) 0.95 (iii) 0.375 (iv) 0.1̇

4. (i) 4% (ii) 5% (iii) 6.25% (iv) 10%

Module 6

Quick test questions

1. (i) 430 (ii) 1100 (iii) 2000 (iv) 8180

2. (i) 1076.1 (ii) 0.0031 (iii) 73.462 (iv) 53.2644

3. (i) 9.3 (ii) 0.004 (iii) 4000 (iv) 84

4. (i) $29.5m^2$ (ii) $30m^2$ (iii) $29.55m^2$

Module 7

Quick test questions

1. (i) 6.95 (ii) 10.81 (iii) 33.43kg (iv) 2.17

2. (i) 45 000 000 (ii) −0.61 (iii) 210 (iv) 7.4

3. (i) $1\frac{3}{10}$ (ii) $3\frac{19}{45}$ (iii) $1\frac{3}{20}$ (iv) $\frac{3}{4}$

4. (i) $4.425\ 659 \times 10^6$ (ii) 2.4755×10^{-1}

NUMBER

Practice Questions

1. a 368, 386, 638 **b** 1 **c** 36, 81

2. a

b 3 **c** 90 **d** $2 \times 3^2 \times 5$

3. a $\frac{18}{5}$ **b** $\frac{5}{18}$ **c i** $\frac{349}{90}$
ii $3\frac{29}{90}$ **iii** 100% **iv** 12.96
d $\frac{5}{9} = \frac{10}{18}$ or $\frac{9}{5} = \frac{18}{10}$ or $\frac{10}{5} = \frac{18}{9}$ or $\frac{5}{10} = \frac{9}{18}$

ALGEBRA

Module 8

Quick test questions

1. (i) x^4 (ii) y^2 (iii) $6a^2b$ (iv) 0

2. (i) a^8 (ii) b^4 (iii) c^6 (iv) d

3. (i) $3a$ (ii) $-b + c$ (iii) $p + 2x + 3$ (iv) $2y + 3$

4. (i) $3a + 12b$ (ii) $-4c - 6d$
(iii) $5x - 5y + 5z$ (iv) $-3p + 3q - 6r$

Module 9

Quick test questions

1. (i) $7a^2 + 8a$ (ii) $6ab + a + b$ (iii) $4c^2 - 2c + d$
(iv) $x^2 + 2x + y^2 - 3xy$

2. (i) $n(m + 3 + n)$ (ii) $4b(a - 2b)$ (iii) $2x(x + 3)$
(iv) $5y(2 - y + 3x)$

3. (i) $a^2 + 5a - 14$ (ii) $b^2 + 5b - 6$ (iii) $9p^2 - 4$
(iv) $4p^2 - 25$

4. (i) $(q + 6)(q - 6)$ (ii) $(3b + 7)(3b - 7)$
(iii) $(5 + 2y)(5 - 2y)$ (iv) $(9 + 11r)(9 - 11r)$

Module 10

Quick test questions

1. (i) $V = w \times 2w \times 3w = 6w^3$ (ii) $C = 35P + 60S$

2. (i) 31.42mm (ii) $38.48cm^2$ (or $38.49cm^2$)
(iii) $137.44cm^3$ (or $137.46cm^3$)
(iv) $113.10\ cm^3$ (or $113.11cm^3$)

3. (i) $w = \frac{P - 2l}{2}$ or $w = \frac{1}{2}P - l$ (ii) $h = \frac{V}{\pi r^2}$
(iii) $h = \frac{2A}{b}$
(iv) $r = \sqrt[3]{\frac{3V}{4\pi}}$

4. (i) 82.4°F (ii) 23.9°C

Module 11

Quick test questions

1. (i) 8 (ii) −17 (iii) $\frac{3}{2} = 1.5$ (iv) 17 (v) 7 (vi) 6

2. (i) $-\frac{1}{2}$ (ii) 3 (iii) 4 (iv) 7

3. (i) 9 (ii) 16 (iii) 11 (iv) 7

Module 12

Quick test questions

1. self-marking

2. (iv) BD = 4cm, DE = 4.1cm, EB = 4.1cm
(v) isosceles triangle

3. (ii) AC = 4.2cm, CD = 4.2cm, DE = 4.2cm, AE = 4.2cm
(all to 1 d.p.) (iii) rhombus

4. (iii) 90° (iv) right-angled triangle

Module 13

Quick test questions

1.
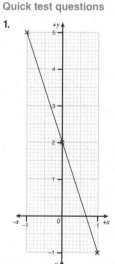

x	−1	0	1
y	5	2	−1

ANSWERS

2.

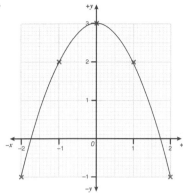

x	-2	-1	0	1	2
y	-1	2	3	2	-1

3.

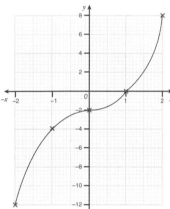

x	-2	-1	0	1	2
y	-12	-4	-2	0	8

4. (i) c   **(ii)** a   **(iii)** d   **(iv)** b

Module 14
Quick test questions
1. (i) 3, (0, 1)   **(ii)** -2, (0, 3)   **(iii)** $\frac{1}{2}$, (0, -2) **(iv)** $\frac{3}{5}$, (0, 2)
2. (i) – (iv)

(i)
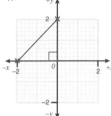

(iii)
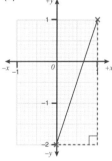

(ii)
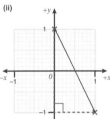

(iv)

(v) same gradient, lines parallel
3.

x	-1	0	1
y	3	2	1

gradient (m) = -1, intercept = (0, 2)
4. (i) $y = 2x + 4$ **(ii)** $2y = 6 - x$ **(iii)** $y = 3x + 1$
(iv) $4y = 3x + 14$

Module 15
Quick test questions
1. (i)

	4x + 3y = 5		
x	-1	0	1
y	3	$1\frac{2}{3}$	$\frac{1}{3}$

	5x - y = 11		
x	-1	0	1
y	-16	-11	-6

(ii)

(iii) (2, -1)
2. (i)-(ii)

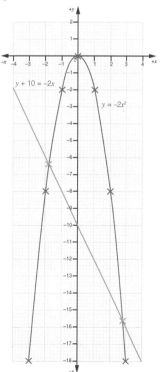

(iii) (-1.8, -6.4); (2.8, -15.6)

3. (i)

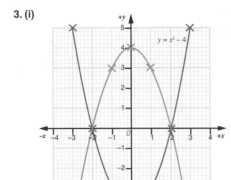

(ii) (–2, 0), (2, 0)
4. (i) See graph above   **(ii)** reflection in x-axis

Module 16
Quick test questions
1. (i) 10secs   **(ii)** 9.2m   **(iii)** 12m
   (iv) 2.9secs, 7.1secs
2. (i) 3   **(ii)** 1500–2500m   **(iii)** 1000m   **(iv)** 40secs
3. (i) Curve with points plotted accurately **(ii)** 60°, 30° **(iii)** 9

Module 17
Quick test questions
1. (i) 16, 14   **(ii)** 55, 66   **(iii)** 243, 729 **(iv)** 3, 1.5
2. (i) 30   **(ii)** 46   **(iii)** 38   **(iv)** 450
3. (i) $n^2 + 1$ **(ii)** $5(n + 1)$ **(iii)** $n^3 – 1$ **(iv)** $26 – 2n$
4. (i) 37, 50, 65   **(ii)** 35, 40, 45
   (iii) 124, 215, 342   **(iv)** 16, 14, 12

ALGEBRA
Practice Questions
1. a $p = 8$, $q = 4$ **b i** $p^2 – q^2$ **ii** 23.56
2. a

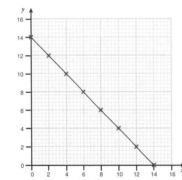

   b –1   **c** –1
3. a

No. of triangles	1	2	3	4	5
No. of straws	3	5	7	9	11

   b add 2 **c** $2n + 1$

RATIO, PROPORTION AND RATES OF CHANGE
Module 18
Quick test questions
1. (i) 2640m   **(ii)** 15.62m   **(iii)** 4m   **(iv)** 27 miles
2. (i) 2ha   **(ii)** $2l$ **(iii)** 6530ml   **(iv)** 103.5l
3. (i) 1.33g   **(ii)** 3200.00kg **(iii)** 2.05kg   **(iv)** 12.14oz
4. (i) 1440mins   **(ii)** 4.17%   **(iii)** 50mins
   (iv) 05:07, 11:30pm

Module 19
Quick test questions
1. (i) 12.5cm   **(ii)** 6.8cm   **(iii)** 2.4cm   **(iv)** 16cm
2. (i) 5.1km   **(ii)** 795m   **(iii)** 11.37km **(iv)** 2.04km
3. (i) F1   **(ii)** D1
4. (i) 066°   **(ii)** 082°   **(iii)** 133°

Module 20
Quick test questions
1. (i) $\frac{60}{500} = \frac{3}{25}$ **(ii)** $\frac{3}{40\,000}$ **(iii)** $1\frac{1}{4}$ **(iv)** $\frac{1}{12}$
2. (i) 1.25%   **(ii)** 11.54%   **(iii)** 3.86%   **(iv)** 150%
3. (i) $\frac{85}{196}$ **(ii)** $\frac{31}{64}$ **(iii)** $\frac{49}{87}$
4. 41.7%

Module 21
Quick test questions
1. (i) 2 : 9   **(ii)** 1 : 4 : 9   **(iii)** 14 : 1   **(iv)** 24 : 10 : 1
2. (i) £135 : £225   **(ii)** 3hrs : 9hrs : 12hrs
   (iii) 10cm : 24cm : 26cm   **(iv)** 140km : 80km : 60km
3. £6000, £15 000, £12 000
4. 200ml

Module 22
Quick test questions
1. (i) £825.30   **(ii)** 10 apples
2. (i) £361.25   **(ii)** £501.60
3. £2831.07
4. (i) £790.50   **(ii)** £820.88

Module 23
Quick test questions
1. (i) 406 miles   **(ii)** 3hrs 27mins
2. (i) 375g flour, 192g sugar, 192g marg., 675g pears
   (ii) 500g flour, 256g sugar, 256g marg., 900g pears
3. £11.60
4. (i) $567   **(ii)** $810   **(iii)** £308.64
   (iv) £216.05

RATIO, PROPORTION AND RATES OF CHANGE
Practice Questions
1. a 0.75kg   **b** 3 : 2   **c** £70.88
   d Shop jumper is cheaper. Quality of knitted jumper is
   known; satisfaction of making knitted jumper.
2. a 52.8km   **b** 33.3cm (1 d.p.)
   c

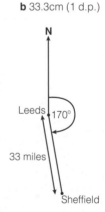

3. a apple 50%, orange 30%, mango 20%
   b apple $1\frac{1}{4}l$, orange $\frac{3}{4}l$, mango $\frac{1}{2}l$
   c 5 : 3 : 2

GEOMETRY AND MEASURES
Module 24
Quick test questions
1. (i) 24cm, 36cm²   **(ii)** 17.8mm, 19.08mm²
2. (i) 29.7cm²   **(ii)** 35.2cm²
3. (i) 64.6m²   **(ii)** 23.1m   **(iii)** £554.40

Module 25

Quick test questions

1. (i) 88mm, 616mm² **(ii)** 82cm, 531cm² **(iii)** 21cm, 35cm²
(iv) 9m, 7m²
2. (i) 16.71mm **(ii)** 4.98cm **(iii)** 8.74mm
(iv) 8.59cm
3. 423cm³
4. 727cm²

Module 26

Quick test questions

1. (ii) 62°–64° **(iii)** AB = 45m, BC = 50m, CA = 30m
2. (ii) ∠PRQ = 89°–91°, ∠PQR = 49°–51°, total = 140°

Module 27

Quick test questions

1. (i) right-angled triangle **(ii)** scalene triangle
(iii) isosceles triangle
2. (i) rectangle **(ii)** rhombus **(iii)** kite
3. (i) octagon **(ii)** pentagon **(iii)** decagon
4. (i) 6 **(ii)** 4, 2, 90° (or right angles)
(iii) trapezium

Module 28

Quick test questions

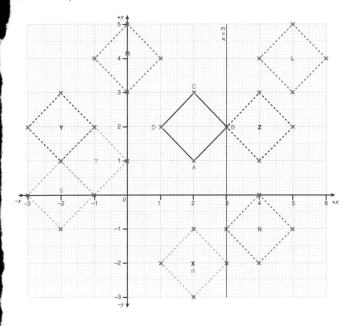

Module 29

Quick test questions

1. (i) SSS **(ii)** RHS **(iii)** SAS **(iv)** AAS
2. (i) $x = 15.4$mm, $y = 6$mm **(ii)** $x = 12$mm, $y = 9.6$mm
3.

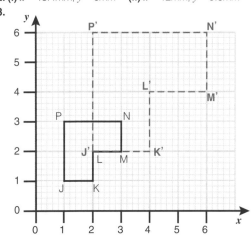

Module 30

Quick test questions

1. (i) b **(ii)** $(a + b)$, $(b + c)$ or $(a + b + c)$ **(iii)** a and c **(iv)** d
2. (i) 50° **(ii)** 55°, 96°
3. $p = r$, $q = s$, $u = w$, $t = v$ (vertically opposite angles)
   $p = t$, $w = s$, $u = q$, $r = v$ (corresponding angles)
   $s = u$, $r = t$ (alternate angles)

Module 31

Quick test questions

1. (i) 14.5cm **(ii)** 13m
2. (i) yes **(ii)** no
3. (i) AB = 22.1 **(ii)** AC = 30.6 **(iii)** ∠C = 25°

Module 32

Quick test questions

1. (i) square-based pyramid **(ii)** cone
(iii) cube **(iv)** triangular prism
2. 37.7cm³
3. SA = 217cm², $V = 254$cm³

GEOMETRY AND MEASURES

Practice Questions

1. a Both are right-angled
   ($25^2 = 625$; $7^2 + 24^2 = 49 + 576 = 625$)
   b e.g.

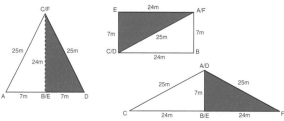

   P1 = 64m, P2 = 62m, P3 = 98m
   c $A = \frac{1}{2} \times 7 \times 24 = 84$m²
   d ∠A = 73.7°, ∠C = 16.3°
2. a 377ml or cm³ **b** approx. 4 **c** approx. 6
3. Accept values ±1 for centre of enlargement

Enlargement	Centre of enlargement	Scale factor
D → E	(3, 29)	2
E → F	(22, −3)	2
F → D	(6, 18)	$\frac{1}{4}$

PROBABILITY

Module 33

Quick test questions

1. (i) unlikely **(ii)** evens **(iii)** impossible **(iv)** certain
2. (i) $\frac{21}{26}$ **(ii)** $\frac{5}{26}$ **(iii)** 1 **(iv)** 0
3. (i) $\frac{3}{6} = \frac{1}{2}$ **(ii)** $\frac{3}{6} = \frac{1}{2}$ **(iii)** $\frac{2}{6} = \frac{1}{3}$
(iv) $\frac{3}{6} = \frac{1}{2}$
4.

Module 34

Quick test questions

1. (i) $\frac{18}{35}$ **(ii)** $\frac{17}{35}$ **(iii)** $\frac{1}{7}$
2. (i) $\frac{1}{4}$ **(ii)** $\frac{1}{4}$
3. (i) $\frac{4}{11}$ **(ii)** 1 **(iii)** $\frac{6}{11}$ **(iv)** $\frac{3}{11}$
4. (i) $\frac{5}{9}$ **(ii)** $\frac{25}{36}$ **(iii)** $\frac{1}{18}$ **(iv)** $\frac{1}{4}$

Module 35

Quick test questions

1. (i) {Jan, Jul}

(ii) {Jan, March, May, Jun, Jul, Aug, Oct, Dec}

(iii)

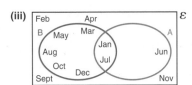

2. (i) {1, 3, 5, 15}   **(ii)** {1, 2, 3, 5, 6, 10, 15, 30}

(iii)

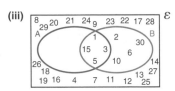

3. (i) Football team 6, swimming team 5 **(ii)** 2   **(iii)** 19   **(iv)** 16

PROBABILITY

Practice Questions

1. a 0.08 or $\frac{2}{25}$ **b** 0.92 or $\frac{23}{25}$ **c** 0.84 or $\frac{21}{25}$

2. a

1↓ 2→	1	2	3	4
A	A 1	A 2	A 3	A 4
B	B 1	B 2	B 3	B 4
C	C 1	C 2	C 3	C 4
D	D 1	D 2	D 3	D 4

b $\frac{2}{16} = \frac{1}{8}$ **c** $\frac{6}{16} = \frac{3}{8}$

3. a i 9   **ii** 5   **iii** 3   **iv** 24   **b** 71

STATISTICS

Module 36

Quick test questions

1. (i) discrete   **(ii)** continuous   **(iii)** discrete   **(iv)** grouped

2. (i)

Eye colour	Blue	Brown	Green	Other
freq (girls)	12	13	3	2
freq (boys)	9	15	2	1

(ii) 30   **(iii)** 57

3. Questions all too open ended. Examples:

(i) How old are you?

≤11yrs ☐   12–14yrs ☐   15–16yrs ☐

(ii) How often do you visit the library each week?

never ☐   1 ☐   2 ☐   3 ☐   4 or more ☐

(iii) Which type of book do you borrow?

adventure ☐   crime ☐   romance ☐ other ☐

(iv) How many books do you borrow in a week?

none ☐   1 ☐   2 ☐   3 ☐   4 or more ☐

Module 37

Quick test questions

1. (i) mean = 31   median = 30.5   mode = 30   range = 19

(ii) mean = 83.9   median = 88   mode = 90   range = 26

(iii) mean = 6.89   median = 7   mode = 8   range = 8

2. (i) mean = £44   median = £42   mode = £42   range = £12

(ii) mean = 85.78p   median = 86p   mode = 83p   range = 7p

(iii) mean = €166.67   median = €169.50   mode = €172   range = €21

3. (i) mean = 52.17cm   median = 52.5cm   mode = 53cm   range = 2cm

(ii) mean = 263.5g   median = 277g   mode = 290g   range = 101g

(iii) mean = 81.67ml   median = 81ml   mode = 81ml   range = 8ml

4. 164.3cm

Module 38

Quick test questions

1. black: 2 pictures   white: $5\frac{1}{2}$ pictures

silver: 5 pictures   blue: $3\frac{1}{2}$ pictures   red: $1\frac{1}{2}$ pictures

2. cat: 135°   dog: 162°

fish: 45°   rabbit: 18°

3. a width = 17–19mm   **b** length = 75–77mm

STATISTICS

Practice Questions

1. a raw data from a survey; data from ticket sales over 3 months

b samples of each age group

c e.g.

i. How old are you?

≤10 ☐   11–18 ☐   19–30 ☐

31–45 ☐   46–55 ☐   56+ ☐

ii. What part of the week do you like to come to the cinema?

Mon–Thur ☐   Fri–Sun ☐

iii. What time of day do you most like to come?

afternoon ☐   evening ☐

iv. What kind of films do you like?

animation ☐   adventure ☐   thriller ☐

comedy ☐   romance ☐   other ☐

v. How did you travel to the cinema today?

walk ☐   cycle ☐   car ☐

public transport ☐

2. a 4   **b** 5.2   **c** 1.3

3. a 25   **b** 53%   **c** 92% – 24% = 68%

d mean = 57%, median = 59%

e Mean is the most appropriate average as it uses all the marks.